Sailboat Projects

Clever Ideas and
How to Make Them
– For a Pittance –

That'll Make You Say:
Why Didn't I Think of That?

by
Clarence Jones

Revised First Edition

Sailboat Projects –
Clever Ideas and How to Make Them – For a Pittance

Revised First Edition -
Copyright © 2013 by Clarence Jones

Published by:

Winning News Media, Inc.

610 Emerald Lane

Holmes Beach, FL 34217-1218

Voice: 941.779.0242

e-mail: cjones@winning-newsmedia.com

ISBN-13: 978-1481924160
ISBN-10: 1481924168

Books by Clarence Jones:

Winning with the News Media - A Self-Defense Manual When You're the Story (Print, 8th Edition)

They're Gonna Murder You - War Stories From My Life at the News Front (both print and e-book versions)

Sailboat Projects – Clever Ideas and How to Make Them – For a Pittance (both print and e-book versions)

Webcam Savvy – For Job or News Interviews (e-book)

Shortcuts for Windows PCs – Wow, I Didn't Know You Could Do That (e-book)

Table of Contents

The First Edition of Sailboat Projects, published in August, 2012, was an e-book that did not contain the last two chapters in this book. They show:

- How to make a swing-out GPS bracket and
- How to install an anchor windlass.

The last chapter in the original e-book (About the Author) has also been edited and replaced in the e-book. The contents of both print and electronic versions are now the same. Both are designated as the Revised First Edition.

The print and electronic versions of the book carry separate ISBN numbers.

Preface

Part of the joy of owning a sailboat for me has always been designing and building upgrades and accessories. Particularly when I can make them for a fraction of what the boating specialty stores charge.

I write. I invent. I tinker. I sail. That's what this book ~~is...~~ ~~...llection of articles~~ that show you how to make upgrades and gadgets for your boat that will enhance your sailing experience.

My sailing started with a 12-footer about 40 years ago. I took lessons at the Coconut Grove Marina in Miami. A string of trailerable boats that kept getting bigger followed. In 2010, living in a canal-front home on Anna Maria Island (in the mouth of Tampa Bay) I moved up to a 28-foot Catalina. Because I was a television investigative reporter for many years, all my boats were named PRIME TIME.

Since I left TV, I've produced several books and a lot of how-to pieces in newspapers and magazines. My guidelines for these DIY projects – and the writing about them – have always been:

- Simplicity
- Ease of assembly
- Minimal cost
- Lots of pictures
- Where to get the materials

Sailboat Projects

The projects in this book vary from very simple (Easier Outboard Shifting) to fairly complex (Mast Raising System, and Custom, Free Navigation Charts). Some of them were previously published in magazines like *Boat Works* and *Good Old Boat*.

Browse through the topics in the Table of Contents. Somewhere in there, you'll probably discover one or more projects you'll want to make for your boat.

Please send feedback when you build a project, particularly if you find a better, cheaper way to do it. I'll update the book to show your improvement.

And tell us about projects you'd like to see us explore. This book will probably have a sequel or three.

Welcome aboard.

Snagging the Dock

I've found an easy way to snag a dock cleat, stop the boat, and tie it securely when I return from sailing.

The secret is a ten-foot length of line. One end is tied to the dock. A loop at the other end has been modified to hang with the loop wide open, ready to be grabbed with a boat hook.

The loop is held in place with Velcro®. When I grab it, the loop comes loose, and I drop it over the boat's port jib winch. That keeps the stern secure while I go forward to grab another post and tie the bow line.

It took several incarnations for it to work the way I wanted.

The size and length of the line depend on the size of your boat, and how much room you'll have for the line to play out before it stops the boat. Smaller line is lighter and easier to fasten to the dock bracket. It gives you more stretch, and a gentler stop.

Making the Bracket

Start by making a bracket that will hold the loop out, hanging wide open. **(shown below, upside down)**

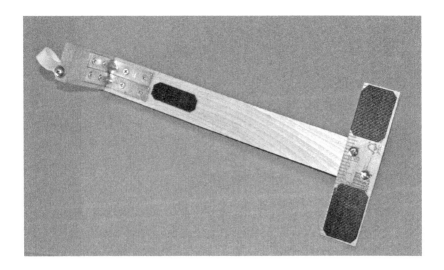

Vertical Piece, Up Close

The vertical piece that slides into the base slot (above) is four inches long.

There's a nylon cable clamp that swivels on the end to keep the bracket in its base. This makes it easy to install and remove when the clamp is swiveled out of the way.

I don't leave the bracket on the dock full-time. Velcro deteriorates in the sun. The two sections of the bracket are connected with corner braces that were coated with poly-urethane to avoid rust.

The first version had brass corner braces, trying to prevent a rust problem. The brass was too soft. It twisted out of shape when I pulled the loop loose from the Velcro patches.

Virtually any kind of wood will work. I first used a wooden yardstick. The yardstick was one-quarter-inch thick and 1½ inches wide. I underestimated the holding power of Velcro. Pulling the line off the bracket bent the brass corner braces, and twisted the wood to the point that I thought it might break.

I eventually settled on one-half by 1½-inch wood. The horizontal section of the bracket that will hang out from a dock post is 12 inches long. This keeps the loop well away from the post.

The six-inch cross piece forms a "T" and suspends the loop. Notice the placement of the Velcro patches. Those on the cross piece keep the loop open. The patch near the corner braces keeps the free line out of the way.

The base (holster) screwed to the dock post is a 3x6-inch piece of ¾-inch wood. It has two strips of that same wood mounted on each side. **(Shown below, disassembled)**

Those strips on each side are covered with a 3x3-inch piece of ¼-inch plywood when the base is completely assembled. To install the bracket, you slide the foot into the base slot, then swivel the cable clamp to prevent the bracket from coming out accidentally.

<u>**Holster and Bracket Mounted on Dock Post**</u>

In its first installation, I mounted the base too low. It worked fine at low tide. But at high tide, close to the dock, the loop was so low I couldn't see it — much less grab it.

Applying the Velcro

Prickly Velcro is on the bracket. Fuzzy Velcro is on the line. That's because the prickly side can sometimes stick to fabric or soft lines. You don't want this line to snag something else accidentally.

Velcro comes in a variety of sizes, colors and strengths. I used "industrial strength" patches on both the bracket and the line.

I cut off the corners on the patches that are on the bracket. This helps prevent peeling. Self-stick mailing labels also have rounded corners, for the same reason. The short strip of prickly Velcro at the opposite end of the 12-inch horizontal portion (near the post) keeps the standing line out of the way.

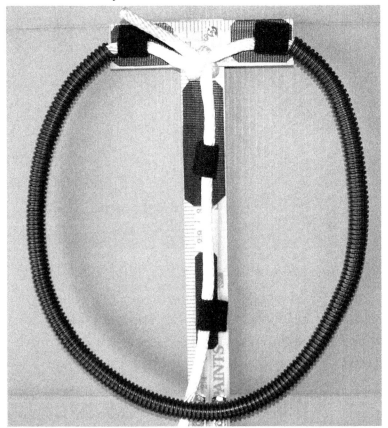

Line Attached to Bracket

The amount of Velcro to use on the line depends on how large and heavy the line is. I used ⅜-inch braided nylon line. My 28-foot Catalina weighs 10,000 pounds. Braided is better than three-strand twist because it offers a better surface for self-adhesive Velcro. Nylon also has more stretch than most line materials.

Velcro has more holding power than I expected. My first try was one-inch wide. It held too tightly. I found a strip of fuzzy Velcro about ½-inch wide and two inches long works well to wrap around the ⅜-inch line.

Notice also that in the early version of the bracket shown above that was made with a yardstick, I had two patches of Velcro. In the later version, I removed the large patch of Velcro you see near the "T". It wasn't needed.

When you wrap the Velcro around the line, let the adhesive sections stick to each other, rather than overlapping. **(below)**

This needs to be done because self-stick Velcro does not hold well on fabric or rope. You can use a bead of hot glue on the edge of the Velcro to make sure it doesn't creep.

My bowline loop is about 10 inches in diameter. I wanted it to be easy to grab with the boat hook. The loop is held open with a length of corrugated plastic cover that's made to protect electrical wires. The plastic cover is split, so it's easy to put on the line. It comes in several sizes and is widely available.

When I sail away from the dock, I put the bracket and line in place, knowing it will be ready when I return. I approach the dock very slowly, put the engine in neutral, then grab the loop with my boat hook. The loop comes free from the Velcro and I drop it over my jib winch.

As the line tightens, the placement of the winch on my boat makes the bow swing in toward the dock. If I put the loop on the aft cleat, the bow tends to swing away from the dock. The spot on your boat where you connect the snagged line will determine which way the bow heads as the boat comes to a stop.

Once the aft end of the boat is connected, I go forward to grab another post, and tie my forward mooring line. If the boat is moving too fast, be careful. A sudden stop can launch you over the side when the aft line becomes taut and stops the boat.

Converting to LEDs

I've converted all the lighting on two sailboats to LEDs, because they use only about one-tenth the battery power of incandescent bulbs.

And the LEDs are brighter. Here's the galley of my Catalina 28 with a strip of LEDs that replaced the original fluorescent fixture.

I'd been thinking about converting for several years, but waited until the price of LEDs dropped, and there was a wider selection. My first conversion was a Precision 21 in 2009. After I sold it a year later, I converted the lights on the Catalina.

When lightning hit the Catalina's mast two years later, it trashed about half of the LEDs. When I replaced them, I was astounded at how many more LED choices were available.

When LEDs were new, many boaters experimented with them and failed, because the LEDs weren't bright enough. Those days are gone forever.

I was able to use all the existing fixtures in both boats. Replacing the incandescent bulbs with LEDs is relatively inexpensive, compared to replacing the fixtures.

Depending on how many bulbs your boat will need, figure on somewhere between $100 and $200 for the total conversion.

Unless you take a lightning strike, the LEDs will last much longer than the boat. They have an estimated life of 50,000 hours. They're very shock resistant, create no heat, and put virtually no drain on a boat battery.

The best place I've found to buy the LEDs (best selection, best price) is http://www.superbrightleds.com. If you go to their website, the number of options is overwhelming. I'll help you navigate the maze.

Your first step is to determine what kind of bulbs are in your present fixtures.

1142 - (left) has a metal base 15 mm in diameter with two contacts. There are two lugs on the side of the base opposite each other, at the same height. The metal base does not conduct electricity. It just holds the bulb in place. The two contacts at the base carry power to the bulb. This bulb requires both a positive and negative wire. Very common in boat lighting.

1156 bulbs have the same 15 mm metal base and lugs, but have only one contact at the base. In cars, the metal body is grounded to the battery, so that any metal in the vehicle can provide the negative contact in a circuit. The base in this bulb is the negative contact. In a car, it eliminates the need for a second wire.

1157 looks like an 1142, with two contacts at the base. But the lugs on the base are offset, one higher than the other. This bulb can only be inserted one way. These are used where a double-filament bulb serves two purposes. The most common use is a tail light/brake light function for the same bulb, with the base as the negative side of the circuit. The two contacts provide two different feeds, so this kind of base would be ideal for an LED that is polarized.

Miniature bayonet base 9 mm in diameter (eight-LED version shown here) with a single contact. The metal base provides one side of the circuit.

Festoon or bullet base. A double-ended, torpedo shape. Often used for boat fixtures because the light can be distributed in all directions. Festoon bulbs come in various lengths and widths. The

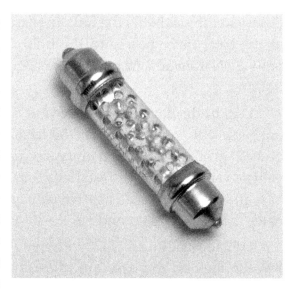

ends of the bulb can fit between spring-loaded contacts or fixed clamps. Some (like this LED bulb above) have a panel that will only shine in one direction. Lots of new LED versions have come to market now with light spreads that range from 90 degrees to a full 360-degrees.

12-volt fluorescent fixtures, which can be replaced by a self-adhesive strip of LEDs that work much better.

Some are Polarized, Some Are Not

Be aware that you will have to match positive and negative contacts in some LEDs. If you turn them on, and they don't light, you probably need to reverse the base 180 degrees to match the polarity of the socket.

Most of them aren't marked, and you can't tell about the polarity of any particular bulb until you try it. I made a testing rig with an old 12-volt DC power brick. To make a tester, cut off the male plug and connect the wires to a couple of alligator clips. Test and mark the positive (red) wire and negative (black) wire. You may also want to check the voltage of the brick. I've found they can be as much as 50% off what they're marked. Many electronic devices (and most LEDs) aren't that picky.

Interior Cabin Lights

Let's start with the easy conversions. Overhead lights in the cabin are fairly standard. Most are circular, five-inch diameter fixtures with a toggle on-off switch on the side.

The light on the left below has been converted to LEDs. The light on the right has its original 10-watt incandescent bulb.

These fixtures usually have an 1142-base, 10-watt bulb. or a festoon bulb (maybe 2 bulbs) of the same wattage.

Ten-watt incandescent bulbs get so hot you can't touch them after they've been burning for about 10 seconds.

There's a great LED solution for dome lights.

17

This small electronic panel about 1½-inches long contains 30 high-powered LEDs. Some panels have 9 LEDs. The panel provides a 120-degree spread of light. They have a universal mini-plug that can connect to a variety of bases.

To make the conversion, all you have to do is remove the incandescent bulb and plug in the LED panel that has the proper base connected. Because they produce no heat, you can just let the panel of LEDs rest on the lens of the dome fixture. If you want to keep it from shifting in a violent storm, use a piece of double-stick tape.

Converting to LEDs

The dome fixtures in my Catalina had two white festoon bulbs and one red bulb. In two areas of the cabin where lighting is more critical, I used an LED panel in both of the white bulb sockets, doubling the brightness.

A simple red festoon LED bulb replaced the old red incandescents. Red light won't zap your night vision. LED bulbs come in a wide variety of colors.

I've found the 30-LED panels are brighter than the incandescent bulbs they replaced. The LEDs draw one watt of power, compared to 10 watts for the original bulb.

In most fixtures that take 42 mm festoon bulbs, you can use a 44 mm bulb. The contacts just spring a little wider. You'll find that 44 mm LED replacements often contain more LEDs than the 42 mm size. So they'll be brighter if you want more light in the fixture you're converting. Two millimeters is about 1/16th of an inch.

The stern light was even easier to convert than the dome lights. I just removed the old incandescent and replaced it with a 44 mm festoon bulb (right) containing four panels with three LEDs apiece. The panels point in four directions, giving the same light spread as the original bulb. And brighter.

Bow Navigation Lights

The red/green navigation lights at the bow are a tad more complicated, because the bulb you should use is counter-intuitive. When you put a white LED behind a red or green lens, the lens filters out most of the light. It only lets the red or green light through, so most of the bulb's brightness is blocked.

This seems to defy common sense, but if you put a red LED behind a red lens, and a green LED behind a green lens, ALL the light goes through. U. S. Coast Guard navigation rules also say the bow lights should cover an arc that spreads 112 degrees on each side of straight ahead. **(below)**

Bow Navigation Light Coverage Arcs

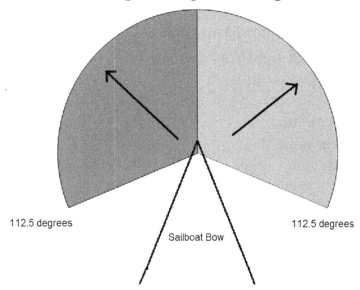

112.5 degrees

Sailboat Bow

112.5 degrees

I used a panel of six very bright LEDs with festoon stubs, top and bottom. The LEDs cover an arc of 120 degrees (slightly more than the Coast Guard requires). My boat carries a separate fixture for port and starboard, which made installing the LED replacements a snap. And the LED panels (below) are MUCH BRIGHTER than the incandescents they replaced.

Testing Brightness

I set up a test board with different kinds of sockets to test the brightness of some of these LED bulbs. Both of the bulbs on the next page were being fed the same voltage and were photographed in very low light.

I cropped the photo of each bulb and pasted them together (sorry, there was another bulb between them that distorted the apparent brightness of these). Remember, the white incandescent on the left had to be seen through a red lens that would filter out the green and yellow contained in its spectrum. The LED on the right emits only red light, so all of its brightness will get through the same lens. The photo replicates very accurately how they appear to the human eye.

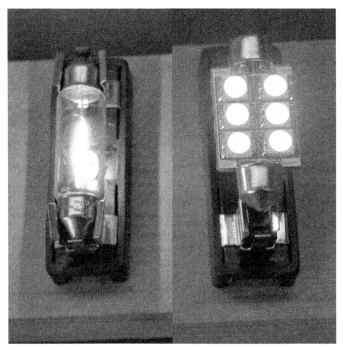

Brightness Comparison

If your bow navigation light is a single fixture that uses one white bulb with a red lens on one side and a green on the other, you may need to be creative.

You may have to use two panels of LEDs, hot-glued at the proper angles, and wired so both panels connect to the positive and negative sides of the original socket.

The same places that sell LEDs also sell pre-wired sockets. The wiring is extremely simple, and there are more varieties of bayonet bulbs than festoon bulbs.

Whether you use festoons or bayonets, make sure you've got red LEDs behind the red lens and green LEDs behind the green lens. If you reverse them, very little light will be visible through the lenses.

Converting to LEDs

Number Determines Brightness

Understand that with LEDs, it's usually the NUMBER OF LEDs that determines how bright the light appears. But some manufacturers' LEDs are also brighter than others. For navigation, go as bright as you can. Cool white will appear brighter than warm white.

Remember - your modification will not be U.S. Coast Guard certified. The rules for boats less than 39.4 feet in length require two nautical miles visibility for white stern and all-round lights; one nautical mile of visibility for red and green bow lights.

You should test your lights after conversion to make sure they conform. Take a witness along. Wouldn't hurt to videotape or photograph the test. Should another boat hit yours, you don't want the captain to claim he couldn't see you because your lights didn't meet specifications.

Anchor Light

One of the major power drains that has always concerned me when we overnight on the boat was the anchor light at the top of the mast. Navigation rules require it to burn all night and have a 360-degree spread of light.

The lightning strike took out both the VHF antenna and the masthead light fixture. The new light fixture I bought contained a squatty (31 mm) 10-watt incandescent festoon bulb.

Before the technician went up the mast to replace the light fixture and antenna, I replaced the original bulb in the new fixture with a 360-degree, 4-LED bulb. These short festoons are hard to find. I bought the bulb at www.yachtlights.com ($14.95).

A Temporary Solution

I had not been willing to go to the top of the mast when I originally converted the lights to LEDs. So until the technician did the work for me, I used a temporary anchor light.

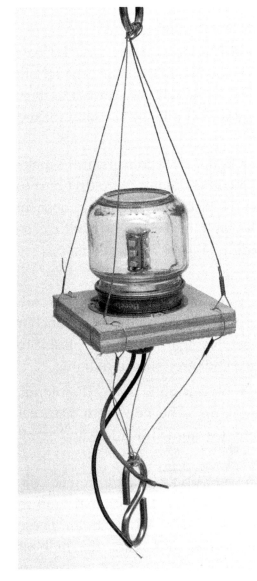

It's an LED bulb that has an 1142 base and 12 LEDs that shine in all directions. I mounted the socket for the bulb in the center of a baby food jar lid. The lid is screwed to a three-inch square piece of plywood. There's a ¾-inch hole in the center through the wood and the lid.

The jar protects the LED from weather. The plywood platform is suspended by fishing leader wire at each corner that connects to a stainless steel S hook above the bulb.

The S was closed by crimping it in a

bench vise. On the underside, the socket's wires were connected to 10 feet of double-strand 16-gauge electrical wire. If you have a trailerable boat the wire from the incandescent masthead light probably plugs into a socket at the base of the mast.

So just put a male plug on the end of the wire from the baby food jar. Or you can power the light with an extension cord from a 12-volt outlet in your cabin.

Get it Back Down

I raised the temporary light with a spare jib halyard. But don't depend on the power wire to pull the light back down, or to keep it in place when it's in use.

If the wire connection should break, you'll have a tough time bringing the light back down. The halyard may be left swinging in the wind, halfway up the mast.

I have a length of dacron line that goes from the underside of the light, along with the power wire. The temporary anchor light can also serve as a deck light if you hang it upside down. Works great.

Fluorescent Replacement

In both the galley and head of *Prime Time*, I replaced the fluorescent fixtures with a 20-inch, waterproof strip of 30 LEDs with self-adhesive backing ($14.95), wired to a simple on-off switch ($1.95).

Installation couldn't be easier. Just peel off the paper strip and stick the lights to a flat surface. Wipe the surface with alcohol to ensure a better grip. You saw the new galley lighting at the beginning of this chapter. On the next page is the head, lighted with the same kind of LED strip.

Head Lighting with LED Strip

I used a shallow electrical box, cut in half, as the container for the small rocker switch to the right of each LED strip.

White Comes in Three Colors

Most white LEDs come in cool white, warm white, or natural white. If you check the specs, you'll find slight differences in brightness. The cool white appears brighter to the human eye, but may not be.

Cool white is very similar to household fluorescent tubes, but in some places can appear too purple. The warm white is closer to incandescent lighting. Natural white is somewhere in between.

I Still Vote for LEDs

LED replacement bulbs aren't cheap. But they cost a lot less than replacement LED fixtures. LEDs are more susceptible to voltage surges than incandescents. But they have a life expectancy of 50,000 hours, and use only one-tenth as much battery juice as an incandescent that's not as bright.

So despite the price and susceptibility to voltage spikes induced by lightning, I still choose LEDs for their brightness and incredibly low power consumption.

In all my years of overnight sailing, I've always been concerned about cranking the engine tomorrow morning.

Sailboat Projects

Easier Gear Shifting

This one is easy. REALLY easy.

One of the most difficult maneuvers for the skipper steering an outboard-powered sailboat is coming into the dock in a stiff wind. On most boats:

- The engine mount sits low and far away from the transom
- The gear shift lever is small and hard to reach
- The stern rail forces you to lean down through the small opening to shift gears
- You can't watch where the boat is heading while you're in that position – unless you're in reverse

When we were tied up after a particularly difficult maneuver, my wife, Ellen, said she thought sure I was going to dive through the stern rail, head first. There was a pause. "Why don't you make an extension for the gear shift lever?" she asked.

Duh. … Brilliant idea.

No more diving through the stern rail opening to fumble with the gear shift lever with one hand, the outboard throttle with the other, losing my cap in the process.

The extension is a 12-inch piece of one-inch PVC pipe that fit snugly over the gear shift lever of our Nissan 6-HP four-stroke. The longer length gives you more leverage and makes the shifting much easier. Notice the notch allowing it to swing past the outboard housing gasket. To keep it securely in place, a stainless screw goes through the pipe, into a factory-drilled hole in the lever that was already there. As though an engineer at the Nissan factory thought: *hmmm — some crazy American might someday want to add an extension for the lever that would make it easier to operate from a sailboat.*

Test the Length

If you make one for your outboard, test the length so the motor will tilt fully with the extension attached.

A coat of black paint from an aerosol can hides its humble beginnings. Cost? About a quarter. Time to make it? Maybe 20 minutes. Works great. **(below)**

Frugal Whisker Pole

When I went shopping for a telescoping whisker pole, I came away with sticker shock. My 28-foot Catalina doesn't really need a monster pole. Just a pole that will hold the genoa out there when the wind behind us needs a little help.

The least expensive ready-made pole I could find online was about $100. Really SERIOUS whisker poles can top $4,000. So I made a light-duty whisker pole for about $50 by modifying both ends of the telescoping handle for a paint roller.

To make one, start by deciding how long you want your pole to be. It doesn't need to be any longer than the foot of your headsail. Shorter – depending on your boat and sail – will probably work well.

Telescoping is always better, because it takes half the storage space, and can be adjusted to sailing conditions. Non-telescoping will REALLY cut your cost.

If you haven't painted a house lately, you'll be surprised at how much telescoping handles for paint rollers have improved. You'll find 4- to 8- foot models, or 6- to 12-foot lengths.

I chose a 4- to 8- foot pole with the larger, handle end of the tubing made of fiberglass.

It seemed stronger and lighter than comparable all-aluminum poles. The locking mechanism was easy to twist and seemed to have the muscle it would need to maintain the set pole length. The pole cost $23 at Home Depot. There were other models for less.

Fittings Online

The best selection of hardware I found for the end fittings was online, at Annapolis Performance Sailing (http://www.apsltd.com). Look in hardware/spinnaker poles and accessories/spinnaker pole end fittings. Many fittings for spinnaker and whisker poles are identical.

The size you buy will depend on the size of your pole tubing. I chose a Forespar clip end ($18) because it fit my extension pole – a one-inch (O.D.) tube that is .9 inches (I.D.). They now sell a kit that includes the clip and a spike end for the same price.

Let's start with the inboard end of my whisker pole. After it's assembled, the module will slip into the handle of the pole.

Here are the parts for the inboard module:

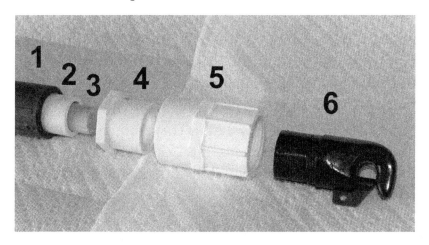

1. The paint roller extension pole handle
2. A four-inch section of ¾-inch PVC pipe
3. A four-inch section of ¾-inch hardwood doweling
4. A ¾-inch to one-inch PVC adapter
5. A one-inch PVC barrel connector, slip at one end, threaded at the other
6. Forespar Lexan® snap-on fitting, (.9-inch O.D.)

All of these parts will depend on the inner diameter of the handle for the pole you select. You may have to be creative to make similar parts fit.

When I cut away the end of my painting pole's rubber handle (#1), I found the inner diameter of the fiberglass pipe was one-inch. So the section of PVC that would slip into that portion of the pole (#2) had to be ¾-inch PVC pipe (about ⅞-inch OD).

The fit was not as snug as I'd like, so I wrapped the PVC pipe with electrician's tape.

Inner Diameters

PVC pipe sizes are INNER DIAMETER (I.D.). But they're not always precise. The I.D. of a threaded female PVC fitting is slightly smaller than the I.D. of a "slip" fitting which is designed to be installed with glue.

As it turned out, my Lexan snap fitting (#6) was so snug inside the PVC threads, it threaded itself into the fitting. I could screw it very tightly into the threaded adapter.

The four-inch piece of ¾-inch hardwood doweling (#3) strengthens the assembly and holds it tightly together, once all the screws are in place.

Tape Makes It Fit More Snugly

To make it fit inside the ¾ inch PVC a little more snugly, I also wrapped the doweling with electrician's tape. With a hammer, I drove the PVC pipe (#2) into the PVC adapter (#4), and then drove #4 into #5. I didn't need to glue them.

With all the parts assembled, I used ¾-inch #8 stainless screws to hold everything in place. All the screws except those that pierce the Lexan fitting reached the hardwood dowel. **(next page)**

Frugal Whisker Pole

I was careful when I drilled into the Lexan fitting to be sure the screws would not interfere with the spring-loaded clip mechanism.

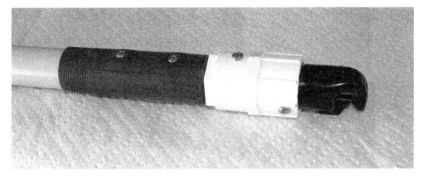

Completed Inboard Module

Now let's move to the outboard, spike module. It screws onto the pole's threaded post.

You'll probably need to build an outboard module for your pole from scratch. Ready-made spike fittings aren't threaded to fit the painter's pole. Here's how I made one:

I found a three-piece wooden paint roller extension set at Home Depot with male threads that screw into female plastic couplers. The three-piece set cost $4. If I messed up, I had spares. **(below)**

The outboard end of the pole could also be another snap-on hook, but it will increase the cost of your parts. I've found the spike is easier to connect and disconnect.

To use the pole, you put the spike through the sail's clew grommet where the jib sheets are attached. With the pole's telescoping friction loose, you clip the inboard end to the mast ring, extend the pole to the desired length, then tighten the telescoping lock and the jib sheet.

First step in building your outboard module is to screw one of the threaded wooden dowels into one of the female plastic connectors and then screw it tightly onto your pole.

Then slide a small piece of one-inch PVC pipe down the wooden dowel until it is seated against the end of the telescoping pole. The PVC pipe will be handling most of the force when the whisker pole is in use.

So you need to measure the distance from where the PVC pipe seats on your pole to the outer end of the plastic coupler, plus one-quarter inch.

Mark the wooden extension and cut the wood at that point.

Then cut a piece of one-inch pipe that length. My distance from the PVC contact point to the outer end of the plastic coupler, plus ¼-inch was 2 ¾ inches.

Push the pipe onto the plastic coupler and threaded wooden stub. You'll find the plastic coupler fits very nicely inside the one-inch PVC pipe.

Screw the plastic coupler onto the extension pole as tightly as you can. You may need to adjust the length of PVC pipe. The wooden stub should be flush with the PVC pipe, or slightly inside the pipe.

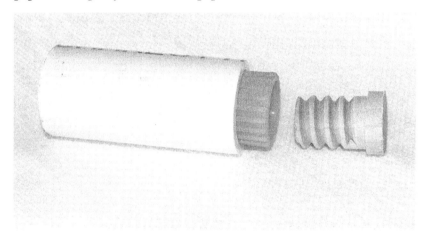

With the wooden stub and coupler screwed tightly onto the pole, you want the PVC pipe to firmly seat against the end of your extension pole.

To make the pipe fit better against my telescoping pole, I used a Dremel® tool to taper the inside of the PVC pipe where it fits against the extension pole.

In use, the force should be on the extension pole, with the PVC pipe pushing against it.

The threaded wood and plastic coupler maintain the connection, but are not strong enough to handle the compression force when the whisker pole is deployed.

To finish the outboard module:

- Drill a one-quarter-inch hole in the center of a one-inch PVC pipe cap

- Insert a 3½-inch stainless, ¼-inch screw into the cap from the inside. The screw will need to be threaded its entire length

- Put a nut on the screw on the outside of the cap and tighten it. Tap the cap onto the PVC pipe

- Make sure the head of the screw is against the wood in the plastic coupler, and the cap is seated on the PVC pipe

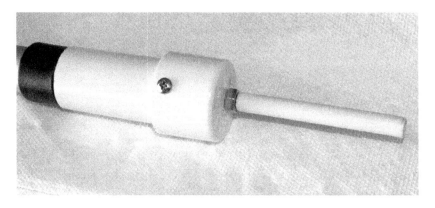

If everything is not in contact, you should adjust the length of the PVC pipe slightly.

Once you're satisfied with the fit, put two metal screws through opposite sides of the cap that are long enough to go through the PVC pipe and into the threaded wood that's inside the plastic coupler.

Frugal Whisker Pole

Use a short piece of ¼-inch (I.D.) plastic tubing to cover the threads of the ¼-inch screw so they won't chafe your sail.

Ring Mounted on Forward Side of Mast

In use, the hook attaches to a ring mounted on the forward side of the mast. The ring set me back $22.

You'll need one of these, no matter what the whisker pole costs. I tapped and threaded the screws that hold the ring in place. Pop rivets would have been easier, but I thought the screws might be a little stronger.

The ring should be mounted so a line between the ring and the clew of your sail is horizontal when the sail is deployed.

I store my pole on deck between two stanchions. It's easy to get to when it's needed. The outboard spike end goes into a line eye that is made to attach to a stanchion.

Pole Spike Held by Stanchion Line Eye

At the other end, the inboard fitting snaps onto a stainless anchor shackle that's held on the stanchion with a stainless pipe clamp.

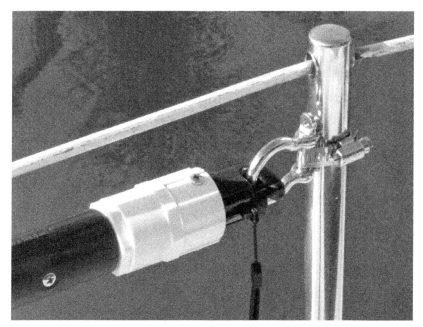

Whisker Pole Storage, Inboard End

Let's go sailing!

Parts Needed for This Project

- Telescoping aluminum or fiberglass paint roller extension pole

Inboard module

- Snap-on spinnaker/whisker pole fitting
- Four-inch piece of ¾-inch PVC Schedule 40 pipe
- Four-inch piece of ¾-inch hardwood doweling
- ¾- to one-inch PVC adapter

- One-inch PVC coupler, slip to threaded
- Four #8 stainless steel screws ¾-inch long

Outboard Module

- Wooden paint roller extension with plastic coupler
- Approximate 3-inch piece of one-inch PVC pipe
- End cap for one-inch PVC pipe
- Quarter-inch fully threaded hex-head stainless steel screw 3½ inches long
- One ¼-inch stainless steel nut
- Four-inch piece of plastic tubing ¼-inch ID
- Six #8 stainless steel screws ¾-inch long

Mast Raising System

With my earlier, trailerable sailboats, I muscled the mast up and down at the boat ramp. But I was a lot younger then. So I built a system that makes it really easy.

You can raise the mast with your fingers. It uses the power of the trailer winch to lift and lower the mast. Total cost? About $50.

I first created this system for a Precision 18. It worked so well, I built another when I moved up to a Precision 21.

This photo shows its fourth incarnation (I no longer own the boat). The primary component is a 10-foot piece of 1¼-inch galvanized plumbing pipe. This creates a high fulcrum point to raise and lower the mast using the trailer winch and its nylon strap. With a slight adaptation, stepping and lowering the mast can even be done single-handedly.

A Crutch for the Mast

First, you need a crutch to elevate the mast at the transom. This will make raising the mast simpler because it gives you a head start. It also gets the mast up and out of the way when you need to work in the cockpit or cabin with the boat on its trailer.

I made the crutch about head-high, with a roller on top, so it's easy to move the mast forward or aft. The higher the better for the crutch, in terms of getting a head-start for raising the mast.

Crutch Base

The crutch is 2x4 lumber with a cross-piece at the bottom. The base rests in the floor of the cockpit at the transom. The base has two slices of one-inch doweling screwed into the bottom.

They're spaced to fit in the Precision's cockpit drain holes. They keep the crutch stabilized extremely well.

If your boat doesn't have drain holes, you'll need to find another way to anchor the crutch in the floor of the cockpit. The base of the crutch should be as wide as the cockpit floor This will help keep it centered and prevent its leaning to port or starboard.

Warning: DO NOT TOW THE BOAT WITH THE MAST IN THE CRUTCH. It's not stable enough to take a hard turn. A pothole could bounce the mast out into the street.

However you design it, stability when the crutch is in place is critical. If the mast should fall, it could cause serious personal injury and/or damage to your boat.

Crutch Roller

There's a rubber roller at the top of the crutch which makes moving the mast forward or aft much easier. At the top of the crutch, I screwed two pieces of 1x2 oak (chosen for oak's strength) to the sides of the crutch to form hubs for the axle.

They had to be shimmed out slightly to fit the four-inch-wide roller. The axle is a ⅜-inch bolt running through a short piece of ½-inch PVC pipe. You won't need the PVC if you buy a larger bolt, but a larger one is not necessary for strength.

The two side pieces of oak had to be cut shorter than I would have liked, to allow the mast shroud fittings to roll past. If your shroud fittings will allow it, leave the oak pieces longer, to give side walls to the roller and more safety in keeping the mast centered on the roller.

Mast Cradles

This system uses cradles built with man-made wood. The cradles do double duty. They hold the mast when the boat is being towed, and they're an integral part of the mast raising system.

The cradle at the stern (below) includes a line to hold the crutch in place and keep it stable when it's in use.

The same line keeps the mast secure when it's lowered and stored in the cradle.

Horizontal Arm for the Crutch

You'll need a horizontal piece of 2x4 lumber screwed into the crutch on the aft side to slide into the cradle and secure it to the stern rail.

A piece of wood screwed to the crutch may also be necessary as a spacer between the crutch and the transom wall at the rear of the cockpit, to keep it vertical.

With the arm in the cradle, the line was wrapped so it kept the crutch from moving forward or sideways.

There's another cradle mounted on the bow pulpit (next page). Both cradles are lined with carpet.

Clamps to Hold the Cradles

They're attached to the bow pulpit and transom rail with plastic clamps that are used to bolt electrical conduit to a flat surface.

If you sail in fresh water, use galvanized clamps rather than plastic. They're much stronger. If you use plastic, check them regularly to make sure they're not showing stress cracks.

Throughout the project, I used either stainless steel or weather-proof deck screws to avoid rust problems.

On one side of each mast cradle, I drilled a hole near the bottom, knotted a short piece of line, threaded it through the wall of the cradle, and installed a cleat on the other side to secure the mast and/or the crutch.

Bow Cradle

The bow cradle is similar to the stern cradle, but is also used as a bracing point for the vertical pipe attached to the trailer. The top of the pipe creates the high point for raising or lowering the mast.

Notice that this cradle is also carpeted, and has a cleat so you can tie the mast securely for towing.

Bow Cradle and Post Brace

The bow cradle has a 2x4 and a one-inch plank attached to the starboard side of the cradle. This is the point where the pipe is braced against the 2x4 to take the load as the mast is raised or lowered. The one-inch plank keeps the post from slipping off the brace.

More on that below, as I write about how to install the pipe on the trailer.

Highway Vertical Clearance

In most states, the law sets vertical clearance for vehicles under wires or bridges at 13.5 feet. Power lines are supposed to be higher.

Attaching the Pipe to the Trailer Tongue

The ten-foot mast-raising pipe, clamped to the trailer tongue, will be about 11 feet high when the trailer is being towed. At first, I cringed each time I passed under a wire strung across the street, But the clearance is deceptive. The lines seem lower than they really are. If a semi-trailer can go under the wires, so can your trailer.

51

The 10-foot galvanized pipe is attached to the trailer tongue with standard galvanized U-bolts and backing plates. A short piece of 1¼-inch pipe with a tee on each end forms a brace between the mast-raising pole and the trailer winch pedestal. (below)

Notice how the ridges at each edge of the galvanized tees form a slot to keep the U-bolts in place.

Experiment to determine how far ahead of the winch pedestal you should mount the 10-foot pipe. The pipe should be vertical and placed so it will touch the bracing point on the bow cradle.

Pole Braced Against Winch Pedestal

Also check the route for the winch strap. It will go to the top of the pipe, then turn aft to hook onto a line that's connected to the mast at a point near the top. From the pedestal brace to the top of the pole is about 8 feet.

Because of that length, the leverage on the pipe when the mast is being raised or lowered is tremendous. Enough to bend the pipe if it's not also braced at the upper end. Positioning the pipe against the bow cradle strapped to the pulpit decreases that leverage.

Pulley Where Strap Angles Toward Stern

At the top of the pipe, I made a pulley where the winch strap goes up, then changes direction and turns toward the boat's stern.

The pulley is made with a galvanized pipe tee, two backing plates, a ⅜-inch stainless steel bolt as the axle, and a piece of ½-inch PVC pipe as the roller for the strap.

Notice the piece of doweling wedged inside the tee, to maintain the angle for the backing plates.

A Line To Handle the Load

I used the jib halyard as the line to raise and lower the mast. The winch strap came up through the roller at the top of the pole, then hooked into the halyard shackle.

If you can't use a jib halyard, you'll need to install a bridle of some kind near the top of the mast, with a line attached. Make sure both the bridle and the line are strong enough to handle the force as the mast is raised or lowered.

Go Gently

With this system, it is extremely easy to raise and lower the mast. My wife cranked the winch while I stood on top of the cabin to keep it centered, and to make sure none of the rigging got snagged on the way up.

Go very gently. The winch has tremendous power, and you can easily break something if a rigging cable gets snagged.

Make sure the turnbuckles at the base of the shrouds are not stuck at an angle, as the mast nears the vertical position. The turnbuckles will bend easily if they're not swiveling freely.

Furler Boot

I also found the base of my CDI Flexible Furler® had a tendency to hang up as it was dragged along when the mast was raised. So I built a furler boot out of a plastic Gatorade® bottle, slit down one side, to cover the furler spool.

Boot to Prevent Furler Snags as Mast Goes Up

The boot snapped on and off easily and was held in place with Velcro straps. It prevented the fitting from snagging on something and getting damaged.

When you lower the mast, make sure the sliding companionway hatch is closed. If it's open, in many boats the forward edge of the hatch is very close to the base of the mast. The mast will come down on it and crack it.

Centering the Mast if You're Single-handed

My P-18 had small stainless eyestraps on each side of the mast, about six feet from the base. Tying a line from each eyestrap to a lifeline stanchion on each side kept the mast centered as it was raised or lowered, enabling the process to be done single-handedly.

If a rigging cable got stuck, you could lock the winch, go up and release the snagged cable, then return to the winch to finish the job.

Without this system, I would have reached the point years ago when I was no longer physically able to raise and lower the mast. This was one of the most useful projects I ever designed.

Materials Needed for This Project

Most of these items for this project are available at any hardware or home improvement store.

Pole Assembly

- One 10-foot length of 1¼-inch threaded galvanized pipe
- Approx. two-foot length of 1¼-inch threaded galvanized pipe for pole brace (Length depends on how close you mount the pole to the winch pedestal)
- Three 1¼-inch galvanized tees
- Six galvanized U-Bolts, backing plates and nuts (to attach pole & brace to trailer). Length of U-Bolts and backing plates depends on width of trailer tongue and winch pedestal
- Two 4-inch stainless ⅜ hex bolts and nuts (for pulley at top of pole)
- One small piece of ½-inch PVC pipe as pulley roller
- Backing plates for roller assembly

Mast Crutch

- One 6-foot length of 2x4 lumber (crutch upright)
- Short lengths of 2x4 lumber (lengths depend on boat dimensions for crutch arm and foot)
- Two 10-inch lengths of 1x2 hardwood (roller hubs)
- Trailer roller slightly wider than your mast
- One 6-inch stainless ⅜ hex bolt, nut and washer for roller axle
- One small piece of ½-inch PVC pipe as axle bushing
- Small cleat and length of ¼-inch line

Mast Cradles

- About 3 feet of 1x6 wood or man-made deck planking (artificial wood won't rot or warp, doesn't need paint)
- Twelve 2½-inch deck screws (to mount sides to cradle base)
- Carpet scraps and SS screws to attach them to cradles
- Six ¾-inch plastic electrical conduit clamps & SS screws
- Two small cleats and length of ¼-inch line

Safe Drinking Water

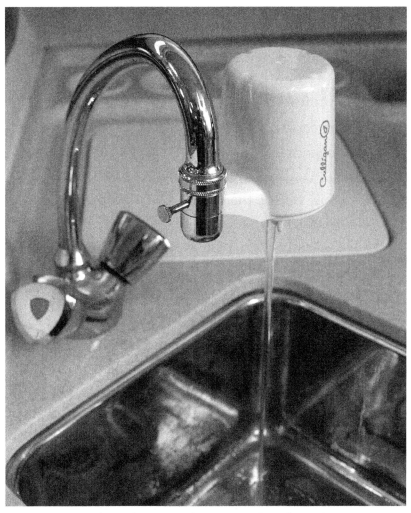

Filtered Water from Sterilized Tank

How long after you fill the tank on your boat with tap water will that water be safe to drink?

When I finally bought a boat big enough to have two showers, two faucets, and tanks that hold 40 gallons of water, I wanted to enjoy that new luxury. But I wondered: How long will the water in those tanks be safe to drink?

I finally came up with the answer after quizzing fellow sailors, studying a bunch of public health websites on the Internet, interviewing the people who supervise water quality at the local utility company, and questioning a university professor.

And the Answer Is …

It all depends.

In most cases, tap water will be good for about a week after it comes out of the faucet. But it depends, among other things, on:

- The sterility of the boat's tank and delivery system
- The sterility of the hose that brings the water to the boat
- The amount and type of disinfectant in the water
- The temperature of the water as it sits in the boat's tank

The difficulty of the question (plus the fear of serious sickness and the terrible taste of chlorine) is why most sailors I know have jugs for drinking water aboard instead of using their much more convenient – and expensive – pressurized water systems.

Some People Barf, Others Don't

One of the significant variables is the immune and digestive systems of those who will drink the water. "I just drain the tank and refill it when the water gets to smelling bad," one boater told me. "I don't know anybody who ever got sick from boat water."

Some Americans drink the water in foreign countries, too, without a problem. Others drink the same water and get incredibly sick. It all depends on their ability to deal with the microbes in the water. Some people could probably survive a cholera epidemic without a burp.

To start my research, I quickly discovered from Internet websites like the Federal Emergency Management Administration (FEMA), the Centers for Disease Control (CDC) and the Environmental Protection Agency (EPA) that tap water, stored in a proper, air-tight container, is safe for at least six months. Maybe longer.

The Two Traps

Uh-oh. Two traps there: PROPER CONTAINER. And AIR-TIGHT.

I also learned that if you're going to lug drinking water onto your boat, plastic jugs that once stored milk or fruit juice are not a good idea. FEMA and CDC agree: "Milk protein and fruit sugars cannot be adequately removed from these containers and provide an environment for bacterial growth when water is stored in them."

I have to assume that water tanks built into boats are "proper containers." But unless they're collapsible, they're not air-tight. Most are rigid plastic (usually polyethylene), and they have to be vented. When water is pumped out, it's replaced with air. The air is the carrier for microbes looking for a place to settle down and multiply.

Tap water in the United States is tested constantly to meet federal standards. The EPA requires that treated drinking water contain at least 0.6 parts-per-million (ppm) of chloramine (chlorine plus ammonia) disinfectant or 0.2 ppm of free chlorine disinfectant (bleach) to kill the microbes that can make you sick. It usually leaves the water plant with a little higher level of disinfectant to allow for dissipation of the disinfectant as it travels through pipes. The farther you live from the plant, the lower the level will be.

Chlorine Dissipates Quickly

But free chlorine dissipates fairly quickly, once it comes out of the faucet. If you place chlorinated water in an uncovered container, the chlorine can be completely gone in 24 hours. Some tropical fish hobbyists make tap water safe for their aquariums just by letting it sit for a couple of days in an open container.

Because of that quick shelf life, about 20 per cent of the public water plants in the United States use chloramines to sanitize drinking water. To create chloramines, they put chlorine into the water, then add ammonia.

The molecules of the two chemicals combine to make a new disinfectant – chloramine. The new molecule doesn't smell and taste as bad as chlorine. And it lasts a lot longer. Chloramines were first used to sanitize public water supplies in this country about 90 years ago.

To find out how your tap water is sanitized, check your water company's annual report. It's a federally-mandated public record, and is probably posted online. My water company (the Manatee County Utilities Department) has been using chloramines for about 30 years.

I met there with Bruce MacLeod, the plant superintendent, and Katie Gilmore, the plant's laboratory supervisor for quality control. They agree that you can safely store tap water in a boat's tank for about a week if the water has been treated with chloramines, BUT . . . **It all depends**.

Temperature is a major factor. At warmer temperatures, chlorine dissipates more quickly and microbes multiply much faster. All microbes won't make you sick. But many will.

To be sure the water in your boat's storage tanks is safe, you'll need a regular maintenance program. It starts with a completely sanitized system. The water doesn't just sit in the tank. It also flows through a pump and lots of tubing. All those need to be clean for really safe water.

The 5-Step Process

Starting with a completely clean system is a five-step process:

- Use a sterile hose to bring the water to your boat
- Sterilize the tank, pump, and all hoses that take water to outlets
- Drain and refill the system with clean water
- Add vinegar to kill the chlorine taste
- Drain and refill with fresh drinking water

The federal CDC recommends a chlorine/water solution of 1/200 (one part chlorine for every 200 parts of water) to sterilize anything that might be contaminated.

Step 1 – The best way to get the water to the boat is through a hose that's dedicated to that job. It's drained and stored when it's not in use. If you want to use any other hose, it will have to be sterilized.

Ordinary garden hoses, you probably know, make water taste terrible. You'll need a special hose made for drinking water. But if the hose has been sitting in the sun for a while, watch what happens when you turn on the faucet.

The first water pushed out of the hose will be yellow, green or brown, depending on how long the water has been there. Just running clean water through the hose won't make it safe. Lots of bad bugs will cling to the inside surface of the hose and contaminate any water that flows through.

A 50-foot length of ⅝-inch hose holds 100 ounces of water. A 25-foot hose holds 50 ounces. To sterilize it, you'll need some fresh liquid chlorine bleach. Make sure it's plain bleach, with no scent or cleaning additive. Don't be tempted to use the old jug of bleach sitting in your garage. It's not dependable. With aging, it loses strength.

For a 50-foot hose, pre-mix ¾ of a gallon of water and a half ounce of bleach in a gallon jug. A 25-foot hose will need half as much. Put the solution aside.

Fill the hose with fresh water, then disconnect it from the faucet. Hold one end of the hose high and drain it completely.

Holding both ends of the empty hose at the same height, pour the pre-mixed bleach solution into one end of the hose. A funnel will help. You'll know the hose is completely full when the cleaning solution overflows at the other end.

Screw the male and female ends of the hose together. This will make a complete, closed loop containing the chlorine/water solution. Let it sit for several hours. Then flush the hose with clean water.

Remember, you can eliminate this sterilizing process if a clean, dedicated hose is stored dry between each use.

Step 2 – Drain the boat's water tank and then refill it halfway. Pour in enough bleach to make a 1/200 solution when the tank is full (about 12 ounces of bleach for a 20-gallon tank).

It's important to add the bleach halfway. Raw bleach is strong stuff. It might damage pump parts. By adding it this way, the bleach will be better mixed when more water is added to fill the tank.

Then rock the boat, or take it for a short cruise to mix the chlorine well. Back at the dock, the next step is one you might not have thought of:

There is old, contaminated water in the pump and hoses leading to each outlet, just as there was in the garden hose before you cleaned it.

Those hoses need to be sanitized. Turn on the system pump and open each faucet or outlet until you smell the chlorine mixture coming through. Be sure to include the hot water heater, if you have one.

It might also be a good idea to remove any shower heads and faucet aerators/strainers. Sludge buildup in your tank and/or hoses could break loose when it's exposed to chlorine, and might clog the outlets.

Water heaters also build up flakes of residue that can clog small openings.

Now close the valves and let the cleaning solution sit for several hours.

Step 3 – Pump it all out and refill with fresh water. Remember to open each outlet so fresh water replaces the chlorine solution in the hoses feeding those outlets.

Step 4 – The entire system will now be clean, but the water will smell and taste like chlorine. To fix that, pour in about a quart of vinegar for every 20 gallons of water. Open the outlets to let the vinegar do its work in the entire system. Then let it sit for at least two days.

Step 5 – Empty and refill the tank and distribution hoses with fresh water. The water in the entire system will now be clean, and should taste just like it does at the tap.

How long will this water be safe to drink? As I said earlier, it all depends. If you don't use it all in about a week, drain the tank and refill it. This will bring in new, chlorinated water to refresh the safety of the tank.

If you're not going to use the boat for at least a week, drain the tank and let it sit empty. Most pumps will leave a little water there. When you're ready to go sailing again, put a couple of gallons of new water in the tank to dilute the leftover residue. Then empty the tank and refill it with fresh water.

At Least Once a Year

Even if you do all this, it's probably a good idea to go through the sanitizing routine for your water system at least once a year. If you really get into this, you might want to do some testing of water stored in your boat's tank for successive days, in both warm and cool weather.

It would make a neat Science Fair project for a teenager to measure both chlorine and bacteria levels daily as the water ages.

Inexpensive kits are widely available to check chlorine content. Your goal is to have a minimum of 0.2 ppm of chlorine or 0.6 ppm of chloramines in the tank. This is below the range of most swimming pool test kits. Be sure to check that the kit will measure the type of disinfectant your water has. If your water company uses chloramines to sanitize the water, you want a kit that can measure "total chlorine."

Bleach for the Long Voyage

For a long voyage where you have no chance to top off the boat's tank, you can add bleach as the water ages. The CDC says clear water can be made safe by adding eight drops of household bleach to every gallon of water. That's a teaspoon for every eight gallons. If the water is cloudy, double the bleach.

The rocking and pitching of the boat will mix the chlorine, but the water will smell and taste absolutely awful. You can fix that with a charcoal filter. They come as a filtering pitcher or a device that attaches to the faucet. The charcoal acts as a magnet to grab and hold chlorine and/or chloramine molecules as the water goes through.

Charcoal Filters for Taste

After studying user reviews of several brands and types, I chose a Culligan® filter for my boat's galley faucet ($28 online, with free shipping and a spare cartridge). It installs without tools and has a five-year warranty. There's a photo of it at the beginning of this chapter.

With this model, the water is not filtered unless you pull a diverter valve. When you turn off the water, the valve springs back to unfiltered mode, like the diverter in a bathtub shower. Each cartridge is good for 200 gallons, but there's no way to measure how much water has gone through the filter.

We use the filter all the time for drinking water, even when we haven't added extra bleach to the tank. Some old salts suggest adding a glass of wine to your boat's water tank to kill the chlorine smell and enhance the taste.

I haven't tried that yet.

Trailer Guides

Trailer guides high enough to center your boat on the trailer and keep the lights out of the water cost about $150 at boating stores.

You can easily make your own for about $30.

Use 1¼-inch Schedule 40 PVC pipe, available at any hardware or home improvement store. To make the guides even stronger, insert a length of 1-inch PVC pipe inside the uprights.

The outer diameter of the one-inch pipe is just under 1¼-inch. So the two sizes fit together nicely, creating a double wall that will be tougher to bend when the wind blows your boat against the guide.

The gray, 90-degree bend is electrical conduit, but is exactly the same dimension as plumbing pipe and will neatly connect to it.

The length of the uprights depends on how high you want the guides to be when the trailer is submerged to launch and retrieve your boat. If in doubt, make them a little high. You can always shorten them later.

PVC Glue Alone Won't Work

When I made my first set of PVC guides years ago, I thought PVC glue chemically welded pipe fittings together. It doesn't.

I discovered this when I looked in the rear view mirror, towing my boat at highway speed. The port side guide (and the light) was bouncing along on the pavement, connected only by the electrical wiring.

The vibration on a boat trailer quickly disconnects glued PVC joints.

So you'll need to use at least two stainless steel #8 or #10 pan head screws to hold every connection together. I use three or four screws at those joints that will have the most stress.

Mounting the guides on the trailer is the only part of this project that may require some creativity. Every trailer is different. Unless the frame of the trailer has a strut that is horizontal to the ground, you'll have to make a tapered shim out of 2x4 lumber to create a horizontal mounting surface. **(see above)**

Use a length of hardwood dowel or galvanized plumbing pipe inside the PVC pipe where long U-bolts will clamp it to the trailer frame. This allows you to put some serious force on the strut without cracking the PVC.

A PVC tee between the horizontal pipe and the 90-degree bend will give you an access port for the wiring.

It's also another way to clamp the assembly so it's sure to remain upright. In this picture, you can see the stainless pipe clamp I used to stabilize the tee against a vertical surface.

At the top of each guide, use a 90-degree elbow and then a short piece of pipe to mount the light.

Remember that you'll need to run a ground wire from the light to a bolt on the trailer frame.

Materials Needed

- About 20 feet of 1¼-inch Schedule 40 PVC pipe
- About 20 feet of 1-inch Schedule 40 PVC pipe
- Two 90-degree 1¼-inch electrical conduit bends
- Two 1¼-inch Schedule 40 tees
- Two 90-degree 1¼-inch Schedule 40 elbows
- About six feet of one-inch wooden doweling
- Four long U-bolts, backing plates, washers and nuts (size depends on trailer frame size)
- Two large stainless pipe clamps
- About 25 one-inch stainless ¾-inch screws
- Wire to extend the trailer wiring up the guides to the lights

D.I.Y. NOAA Charts

The introduction of waterproof nautical charts was a great improvement for sailors. But their size makes them incredibly difficult to handle out in the cockpit in a stiff breeze. And they're expensive. Usually about $20 to $25 each.

For less than $2 per page, you can do it yourself – make your own, customized, waterproof charts for the area you sail. I print mine in 8½ x 11-inch size, and bind several together for stretches of the Gulf Coast where I sail. They're easy to store and much easier to use than the store-bought kind. Even in a rough wind. **(below)**

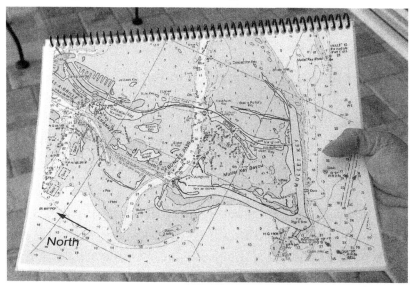

The U.S. National Oceanic and Atmospheric Administration (NOAA) creates the charts. They're public property. The charts you buy at boating stores are made by companies who get these same charts from NOAA. All the NOAA charts are available for viewing online – more than a thousand of them. They're updated every week. The chart you buy in a store could be several years old.

If you have a GPS device on your boat, you should never sail without a printed chart of the area as a backup. GPS screens can never be as detailed as these charts. And electronic devices have been known to fail.

Another idea: If your cell phone or tablet computer has GPS capability and you're close enough to shore to be in range of cell phone towers – you can get a small-screen view of where you are even if you don't have GPS instrumentation on your boat.

There are specialized apps to utilize this capability. Regular GPS devices make a direct connection to the navigational satellites out in space and are not dependent on cell phone signals.

The only shortcoming for printing your own charts is that they will not be printed exactly to scale (like miles per inch).

But you can see water depths, obstructions, landmarks, bridges, etc. exactly as you would on a clumsy, store-bought chart.

The exact distance between two points on the chart may be a little more difficult to determine exactly. I'll explain how to minimize that issue later in this article.

I live on Anna Maria Island at the mouth of Tampa Bay. I'll use that area of the Gulf Coast to show you how to print your own charts. Let's get started.

Online, go to http://www.nauticalcharts.noaa.gov/

D.I.Y. NOAA Charts

Choose View NOAA Charts – U.S. Waters and you'll jump to:

http://www.nauticalcharts.noaa.gov/mcd/NOAAChartViewer.html **(below)**

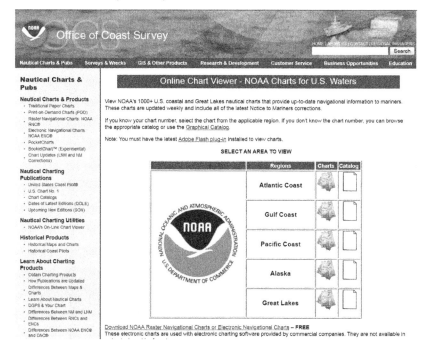

Choose an Area of the U.S.

Choose the area you're interested in by clicking on the Charts icon in the third column – either Atlantic Coast, Gulf Coast, Pacific Coast, Alaska or The Great Lakes.

That will take you to another web page where the charts will be shown in a long list, by number and the area covered.

If you already know the number of the chart you want to print, just scroll down to that number and open the chart.

Gulf Chart Catalog: Chart Side

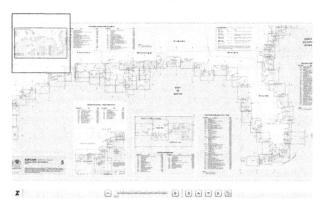

I chose the Gulf Coast (above).

If you don't know the number of the chart you want, you'll see a slot in the webpage table called CATALOG.

If you click there, you'll jump to a large map of the coastal area you chose.

At the bottom of the map is a control panel to help you navigate the page.

You can zoom into the map, then move in any direction, using the control arrows.

When you zoom into the area you're interested in, it will show all the charts that cover that area. **(next page)**

Gulf Chart Catalog: Chart Side

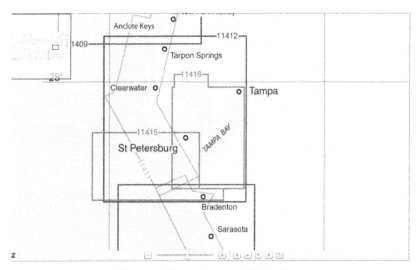

Charts That Cover This Area

Each of these rectangles is a different chart. Notice that each rectangle has a number.

Decide which chart you want and then go back to the previous screen, click the charts icon for your area, and scroll down to that number.

Click on the number link and the chart will appear on screen. The entire chart, if printed to the original scale, would be two or three feet wide.

I chose Chart 11412. It's on the next page.

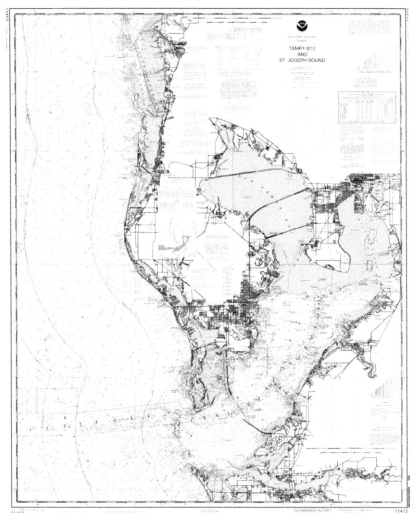

This Chart Would Be About Three Feet Across

The next steps are important. You only want to copy a very tiny section of this chart, enlarged so it's legible.

So you'll need to fill your computer screen with just that section so you can print it on a letter-sized piece of paper.

Because the NOAA website has its own controls to enlarge the chart and move around in it, some of the standard methods for doing this with your keyboard or mouse don't work the way you'd expect them to.

Your Browser May Seem Dysfunctional

For instance – when a web page loads, you can normally touch the F11 key to get rid of all the stuff at the top and bottom of your screen and have only the contents of the page showing.

But if you've already played around in this chart, the F11 key won't work any more. So the sequence below is important.

- With the page loaded, hold down your Control Key and then roll your mouse to enlarge the page until it reaches both sides of your screen.

- Touch F11. All that stuff at the top and bottom of the screen will disappear. It's called a full screen view. You can now zoom and move around in the chart in a number of ways.

- You can use the plus, minus and control features built into the page. Or –

- Left-click anywhere on the page and you'll zoom in.

- Hold down your left mouse button and then moving the mouse takes you around in the chart, just like a Google map.

- So zoom and move around until the area you'd like to print fills the screen.

- Touch the PRTSCR key on your keyboard. This will copy what you see on your screen into your clipboard. Now you'll find that touching F11 won't work. You won't be able to get back to a normal screen so you can print what you've copied. Unless you know how –

- Move your cursor to the side of the screen and right-click anywhere. A drop-down menu will appear. One of the choices is RELOAD. Click on RE-LOAD and your browser will return to the screen as it was before you started zooming and sliding around. Now touch F11 and you'll return to a normal screen with all the stuff at the top and bottom of the page. Or –

- Move your cursor all the way to the top of the screen. An action bar will drop down. Right-click in it and one of your choices will be EXIT FULL SCREEN. Left-click that and you'll be back to normal.

If you want to cover 20 or 30 miles of coastline, you'll need a series of contiguous pages to make a booklet. The more you've enlarged that section of the chart, the more pages you'll need.

Printing and binding them will be your last step. Be sure to read the instructions below on maintaining the same proportions if you print a series of pages from the same chart.

Here are several ways to copy and print your personalized chart pages:

Using a Word Processor

Open a blank page in your word processor. Reduce the margins to ¼-inch on all sides. Change the format from portrait to landscape (landscape means the page is wider than it is tall) because most NOAA charts (and your monitor) are in landscape proportion.

Paste the chart image that's in your clipboard into the blank document. You can do this several ways:

Click the PASTE icon or

Click EDIT/PASTE or

Touch CTRL/V

The chart image will be pasted into the blank page of your document. It will fill the page. Name the file to save it. Then you will be able to print it.

A Much Better Way

Launch a photo editing program such as Adobe Photoshop Elements. Click FILE/NEW/BLANK or FILE/NEW/IMAGE FROM CLIPBOARD. Once you've got the image onscreen, tell the program to make the photo 8 x 10.5 inches at 300 pixels per inch.

When you're happy with the way it looks, touch FILE/SAVE AS and name the image as a JPEG photo file, with maximum quality. Remember in which folder you place it. This technique will give you a MUCH higher quality print than the word processor technique.

Which Way is North?

Some of the charts I created follow a coastline that runs north and south. So NORTH is often to the left as you look at those charts. Since printing a portion of the

81

chart will not include the compass rose, it's important to add an arrow and the word NORTH somewhere in the chart to show which way the chart is oriented. **(below)**

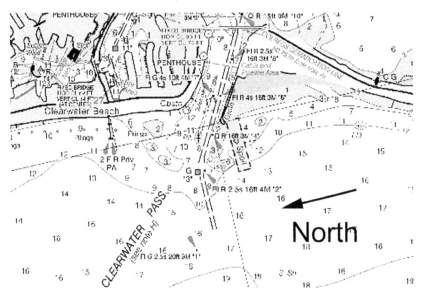

Copying a Series of Charts

When you choose to copy several contiguous sections on screen, let your sections overlap slightly. As you move from one page to the next on your boat, it will be easy to see that one page is contiguous to the next.

If you print several pages from the same chart, you need to keep the zoom size EXACTLY the same from one page to the next. Here's how:

Open the program where you're going to paste and print these chart images. Then use your browser to find the chart, zoom in, and locate the area you want to copy.

After you touch PrtScr on the first page, hold down the ALT key and touch the TAB key. You can then leave your web browser and work in the program where you're going to paste the image in your clipboard. This leaves your browser window waiting exactly as you left it. After you've done the pasting in the other program, use ALT/TAB to go back to your browser showing the chart.

If you move around in it now, be careful not to zoom. When a contiguous area is onscreen, touch PrtScr again, then ALT/TAB back out to paste the second image in the other program.

Include the Chart Scale

Include as one of your pages the chart Nautical Miles scale, **making sure the zoom level on screen is the same** as the other sections you've copied from this chart. If done carefully, this will give your charts a fairly accurate way to determine distance.

The inches on the scale will not be an inch, but whatever their length, they can be used as a unit of measure. **(below)**

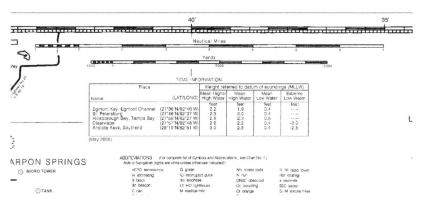

Repeat these steps until you're finished copying and pasting all the pages you want to print. Then normalize your browser window with either Step 8 or Step 9 above.

Printing Your Charts

Use a color printer, and choose the highest quality possible (best photo, or maximum dots per inch). Use glossy or satin-finish photo paper rather than ordinary paper.

The difference in quality between photo and regular paper is striking. Use normal weight photo paper. Very heavy paper will not laminate as well as paper in the 40- to 60-pound range.

Laminate Your Charts

Take the prints to an office supply store. They will laminate them for you, making them rigid and completely waterproof. In my area, the cost is $1.00 to $1.50 per page, depending on the thickness of the plastic laminate.

So the cost of paper, ink, and the lamination will come in under $2.00 per page for letter-sized prints. Larger sizes cost more, and they're also more difficult to store and use when you're sailing.

Binding Your Charts

I've printed a series of charts this way (shown at the beginning of this chapter), to use when we cruise up and down the Gulf coast within 75 miles of home.

After the laminating, the office supply store will do the binding for you, at a very low cost. I like a plastic ring binding that won't rust or corrode. You can turn to any page and it will stay there, lying flat.

A Navigation Safety Warning

All NOAA charts have a section, usually in one corner, that tells you the scale of the chart in nautical miles per inch. The scale varies between charts. Because you have zoomed in on a chart, your printed version HAS CHANGED THAT SCALE. The charts you print will contain the very latest data that NOAA has, but:

THEY SHOULD NOT BE USED FOR NAVIGATION FROM ONE POINT TO ANOTHER WHERE DISTANCE IS A CRITICAL FACTOR IN THAT NAVIGATION.

The companies that sell NOAA charts have more sophisticated methods to reproduce them and maintain the scale accurately. In this smaller size, they're really handy to show depth, landmarks on shore, bridges, marinas, etc.

No matter how careful you were in reproducing the mileage scale, just don't depend on them to show precisely how far away things are.

Sailboat Projects

A Better Ladder

Most sailboats are built with terrible boarding ladders. For those who are not athletic, they can be impossible. The most common problem is ladder rungs of stainless steel tubing. Slippery and painful for bare feet.

The easy solution: Add treads of man-made deck planking. **(below)**

Regular wood will do, but the man-made product has several advantages:

- Its rough surface doesn't get slippery when it's wet
- It doesn't need to be painted or varnished
- It's easy to cut and drill

Start by measuring the diameter of your boarding ladder tubing and the exact inside distance from one side to the other for each rung on the ladder. Decide how wide you want the treads to be.

When the ladder swings down, you don't want the treads striking the boat transom. And the wider they are, the more leverage you exert to rotate them on the rung when you step on the tread. About three inches, front to back, is ideal.

The Cutting Pattern

Draw your treads on the lumber like this. **(below)**

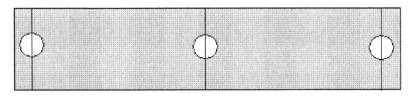

The centers of the holes should be as far apart as the center of the upright pipes on the sides of each rung for which you're making a tread. If your ladder is slightly tapered, each tread will have to be a different length.

Then use a hole saw to cut the holes slightly larger than the ladder tubing. Saw through the holes after the circles are cut, and the treads are ready to mount on the rungs. The notches on each end are necessary to help hold the tread horizontal when you step on it.

With the tread in place, slip two nylon electrical conduit straps around the rung on the underside, then drill and fasten the straps with three-quarter-inch #10 stainless steel, pan head screws.

Straps made for half-inch conduit are perfect for one-inch ladder tubing. They need to be fastened very tightly to prevent the tread from rotating. Three-quarter inch conduit straps will let the tread slip. Use plastic. Metal straps will quickly rust.

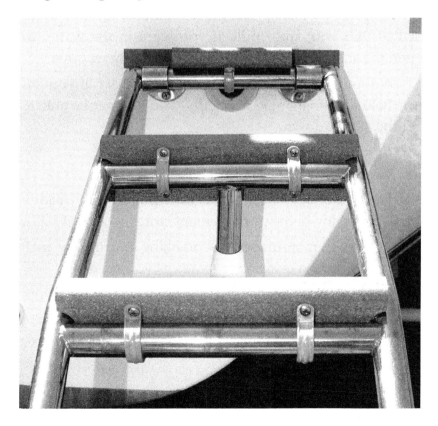

Notice that my top tread is different. It's longer and wider, and held in place by a strap on each side and a third on the aft side of the tread. The tread is also notched to permit the ladder to swing upright to its stored position.

If the bottom rung on the boarding ladder is circular, you may have to stack two or three short pieces of lumber under the tread to reach a point where the notches will hold the tread properly. My ladder came with a plastic tread that I left in place.

A safety suggestion – If your ladder swings up and is held in place by a snap shackle (as mine is) attach a piece of line that you could pull, if you were in the water, to open the shackle and permit the ladder to swing down.

Without the line dangling behind the boat, if you fall overboard sailing single-handedly, you'll never be able to get the ladder down.

Resources Needed

The materials needed for this project are readily available at any home improvement store:

- Enough man-made deck planking approx. one inch thick to make as many treads as you need
- Two nylon electrical conduit straps per tread (½-inch conduit straps for one-inch tubing)
- Two #10 stainless steel ¾ inch pan head screws per strap

Burglar Alarm

The battery-operated, wireless burglar alarms widely available now for doors and windows can provide an easy, inexpensive way to protect your sailboat. They're easy to install. This one protects my Catalina 28.

The wood on the left in the photo on the previous page is the top slat in the companionway. A self-adhesive strip of Velcro holds the magnet in place.

The alarm itself is on the right, also held by Velcro.

Better Than a Lock

I think an alarm is a much better solution than a lock. A serious thief can do serious damage getting into your boat if the cabin is locked. Both serious and spur-of-the-moment thieves will likely move on to another boat if they see a sign warning that your boat has an armed alarm.

When a door, window or hatch is closed, a magnet is positioned close to the spot on the alarm where the internal switch is located. The magnet keeps the switch open.

Opening the door, window or hatch moves the magnet away from the switch. It closes, and that triggers the screeching alarm.

Motion sensors that trigger an alarm won't work for a boat that's afloat. The constant motion will cause lots of false alarms.

Magnet vs. Push Button

Other types of alarms use a push button switch, which requires contact. When the door or hatch is closed, the button is pushed in and the circuit is open. Like the buttons that control car and refrigerator door lights.

When the door opens and the button pops out, it closes the circuit and turns on the light or the alarm. After experimenting, I found the magnet type much better for boats.

Some examples of simple magnetic switch alarms and approximate prices (shop – they vary widely) are:

- Doberman SE-0101 – $11
- Doberman SE-0205 – $20 (shown above)
- GE 45115 –$6
- GE 45117 – $16
- Intermatic SP-440B – $6

All widely available online and in hardware and home improvement stores. All come with double-sided self-adhesive tape to fasten the components permanently in a home to a window or door, and to its frame.

A boat is different. Depending on your boat, the companionway slats may be configured so you have to remove and replace the magnet and alarm components every time you use them. So use sticky-back Velcro instead of the self-adhesive tape.

With the simplest alarms, you'll stick the alarm at the bottom edge of the top slat in your companionway. Then use Velcro to attach the magnet to the top edge of the slat just below. The placement of the Velcro on both slats makes it easy to put magnet and alarm in the right position for them to work properly. You can even do it in the dark.

You put the alarm and magnet in place, turn it on, and slide the hatch cover closed. If a thief opens the hatch cover and starts to remove the top slat, that triggers the alarm.

IT'S A GOOD IDEA TO MAKE A WARNING SIGN. The notice that the alarm is armed will scare off most thieves. But you'll need it, too. Without it, you'll probably forget and set off the alarm the next time you start to enter the cabin.

I printed my sign on heavy card stock, then weatherproofed it on both sides with two-inch transparent packaging tape. It originally sat between two of the companionway planks (below). I later had it laminated and screwed it to the slat.

There are some major technical differences to consider between alarm models, as well as the way you install, arm and disarm them. You'll be happier with the result if you choose an alarm that fits your boat and the way you use it.

Batteries

The Doberman SE-0101 and the GE 45115 use "button" or "disk" batteries, which are expensive, have a shorter life, and provide less muscle than AA or AAA batteries.

The GE 45117, rated at 120 decibels (db), is louder than the others in this group and uses three AAA batteries.

The GE 45115 is also rated at 120 decibels. But if you quickly close the hatch when the alarm sounds, it silences the alarm. Most alarms will continue to screech, once triggered, even if the hatch is closed. Or until you turn them off.

The Intermatic SP-440B is rated at 90 db and uses one AA battery.

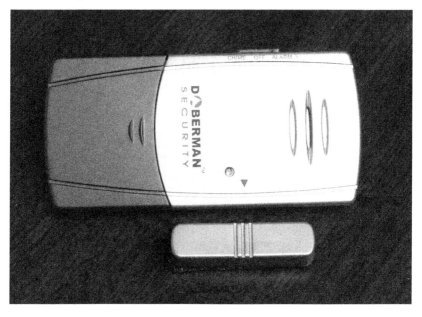

The Doberman SE-0101 **(above)** rated at 95 db, is the smallest and lightest alarm I tested.

Notice the on/off switch at the top of the alarm. If you put the alarm at the bottom of the first slat and the magnet at the top of the second slat (the little arrow tells you where to place the magnet) it's easy to reach down and use the switch after you slide the companionway hatch cover out of the way.

I used this alarm on my Precision 21, but chose another model when I moved up to my current Catalina 28. The design of the Catalina is ideal for not having to remove the alarm when I open the cabin. More about that later.

Most of the units will beep or flash periodically when the battery needs to be replaced. Some have a button to test battery condition.

Immediate or Delayed Alarm

In choosing an alarm, think about whether a delay between the time the companionway slat is moved and the alarm sounds is a good thing. It's convenient, for you to disarm it, but a cool, experienced thief might use that time to defeat the alarm.

When they're turned on, the Doberman models, the GE 45115 and Intermatic SP-440B go off immediately if the alarm and magnet move apart. There's no keypad, and no code to arm or disarm the alarm. Each has a simple on/off switch.

To arm these, put your companionway slats in place. Then stick the alarm and magnet to the Velcro, reach down with the companionway hatch open, and turn the alarm on or off. Then slide the hatch closed.

The GE 44117 gives you a choice about the delay, but there is no quick on-off switch. To set or disarm the alarm requires punching in a four-digit code of your choice. Probably too complicated for most boat uses. It has two modes:

- "Away" gives you 45 seconds to place the two components together after you've used the code to arm it; and 30 seconds to turn it off when you return to the boat. You can move the alarm away from the magnet and use that delay time to input the four-digit code.

- "Home" mode has zero delay before it goes off. You use the keypad to arm it, with the alarm and magnet placed side by side. If the magnet moves, the alarm sounds immediately. In this mode, you'll have to punch in your code with the alarm in place before you remove the companionway slat to prevent the alarm from sounding.

Alarms that require a code would be much more difficult to use at night.

The GE 44117 is larger and heavier than the others. My tests show its magnet is stronger, and doesn't have to be as close to the alarm when it is in operation. The instructions say it can be up to ½ inch away from the alarm case.

Remote Control

I tested alarms to write an article for *Good Old Boat* magazine. The one I chose for my current boat (shown at the beginning of this article) is the remote-controlled Doberman Tool Box Alarm SE-0205 ($20 online, $15 at Home Depot).

It uses a magnet switch at the end of a wire leading to the alarm, rather than having the switch built into the alarm itself.

Remote Control for Doberman SE0205

This makes placement of the switch on the companionway slat much easier. The lightweight magnet and switch are less likely to be accidentally dislodged from the Velcro.

And – depending on the way your companionway is built – the alarm may not have to be moved each time you place or remove the slats.

If the magnet is not placed properly, you get a three-beep signal when you touch the ARM button.

With loudness rated at 100 db, the SE-0205 uses three AAA batteries. The remote works like a garage door remote. No code to remember. No delay. Just touch the remote's "arm" or "disarm" button.

While I would prefer not having to keep up with the remote, I found this model best for me because of its convenience, loudness, batteries and wider choice of ways to mount the alarm and leave it there.

I remove the magnet when I open the cabin, and store it beside the alarm on the Velcro strip there. The batteries last about two months, then have an intermittent beep to tell you they're dying.

One of these days I'll find a way to reduce the voltage at that point and wire the alarm into the boat battery. The AAA batteries will no longer be needed. That's another job to put in the next edition of Sailboat Projects.

Sailboat Projects

Tiller Tender

I've come up with a tiller extension/tender that works on either side of the boat. You don't have to cut into your fiberglass, as you do with some expensive, commercial versions.

Mine is light, won't rot or corrode, and doesn't need any kind of finish or maintenance.

Cost? About $2. If you're a fix-it, do-it-yourself kinda sailor, maybe nothing. Most of the parts are already in your workshop. Time to make it? Less than an hour.

The Extension Rod

The tiller extension is a piece of ¾-inch PVC pipe with a long quarter-inch screw through one end. The length depends on the size of your boat and what you'll connect it to at the other end.

Start by drilling a 3/8 - inch hole vertically through the tiller, where you want the extension to connect. Mine was at a point abeam the aft rail stanchions on a Precision 21.

Cut a piece of ⅜-inch copper tubing as long as the tiller's height at that point. Drive the copper tubing into the hole.

The inner diameter of the tubing is exactly right to serve as a metal bushing for a quarter-inch screw and to prevent the screw from eroding the hole through the tiller. **(below)**

The nut holding the screw in the extension pipe is wrapped in Teflon tape to keep the swivel smooth and to avoid any chance of scratching the tiller. The extension pipe is in two pieces, connected with threaded adapters.

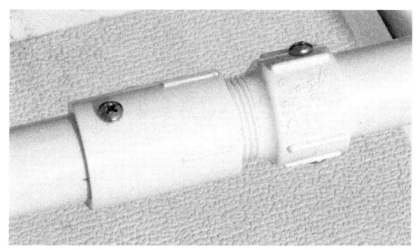

The shorter length works great for relaxed, manual steering from the cockpit seat. But it needs to be longer to reach the fitting that will hold the tiller in place while you do something else.

Notice that the adapters are secured to the pipes with screws, rather than PVC glue.

PVC glue will not hold under a lot of stress and vibration. I write about the painful lesson that taught me this in another chapter in this book that shows how to build trailer guides.

The Tiller Tender

To connect the tiller extension to the stanchion, I started with a piece of one-inch, man-made wood three inches square. I like artificial wood because it's easy to work, needs no finish and won't rot or weather.

To the backside of the wood I screwed two nylon clamps made for ¾-inch electrical conduit. In use, the screws are not quite tight.

This permits the wood to rotate. A stainless pipe clamp around the stanchion sets the height, so the tiller extension will stay horizontal.

Adjustable Clamp on the Stanchion

On the forward side of the wood, I fastened another conduit clamp. This one is adjustable, so you can clamp the extension pipe in place when you've set the tiller where you want it.

The lower hole in the clamp (not visible from this angle) is fastened to the wood with a ¾-inch #10 stainless screw.

A stainless ¼-inch carriage bolt comes through the wood from the back side and goes through the upper hole of the conduit clamp. Hammering the bolt in from the back side prevents it from turning when you tighten the tender's wing nut.

On that screw above the clamp, I added a nylon spacer and a wing nut. The spacer is necessary to turn the wing nut and clear the pipe clamp. A glob of caulk or hot glue on the end of the screw will keep the wing nut from vibrating off.

To use the tiller tender, screw the two pieces of pipe together. Then push it through the clamp that's fastened to the rail stanchion. Drop the screw on the other end into the hole in the tiller, and you're in business.

Adjust where you want the tiller to be held, tighten the wing nut, and you can relax or do something else on the boat.

PVC fittings are not made to rocket science tolerances. If the clamp holding the PVC pipe won't hold it tightly enough, dig a shallow trough under the other end of the clamp that is held down by the #10 screw.

The wing nut will then keep the extension as secure as you'd like.

Materials Needed

- Three-inch square piece of man-made wood
- Three nylon pipe clamps for ¾-inch conduit
- Five #10 stainless steel screws ¾-inch long
- One ¼-inch stainless steel carriage bolt 2½ inches long
- One ¼-inch stainless steel wing nut
- One ¼-inch nylon spacer ¾-inches long

Materials Needed (continued)

- One stainless steel pipe clamp
- About six feet of ¾-inch Schedule 40 PVC pipe
- One ¾-inch PVC pipe cap
- One female threaded ¾-inch PVC pipe adapter
- One male threaded ¾-inch PVC pipe adapter
- Two #8 stainless steel screws ¾-inch long
- Short piece of ⅜-inch copper tubing
- Nylon washers to protect tiller finish
- One ¼-inch stainless screw long enough to go through both the tiller tender and the tiller

Swing-Out Bracket

GPS chart plotters are often designed for bulkhead mounting. But if they're visible, thieves LOVE them. So I made a bracket to swing mine from inside the cabin for storage or into the companionway for use.

In the cabin, it's hidden and out of the weather. In the companionway, it's easily adjustable for maximum visibility.

The cost? About two dollars.

The bracket is made entirely from PVC pipe and hardwood dowels, plus a small wooden platform for the GPS device. And it has a locking system to keep it where you swing it.

View Inside the Cabin

This is what it looks like inside the cabin. That round plastic thing above the bracket covers the back side of a depth sounder/knot meter.

You'll need to measure the space you have between the side of the cabin and the companionway opening.

The length of the primary arm and the height of the wooden platform on which you mount the GPS device will depend on that space.

Ideally, when it is swung inside the cabin, it will be a full, 180-degree swing, which puts the entire assembly out of the way for storage.

The sockets holding the one-inch vertical dowel which serves as the hinge are one-inch pipe couplers.

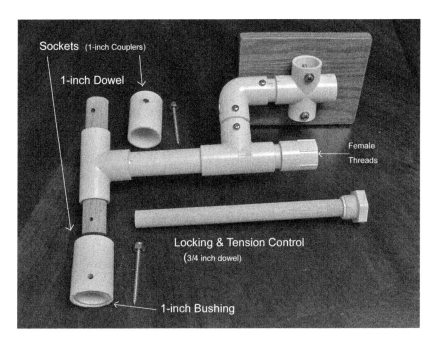

Sockets (1-inch Couplers)

1-inch Dowel

Female Threads

Locking & Tension Control
(3/4 inch dowel)

1-inch Bushing

Some Part Lengths Depend on Swing Arc

At one end of each coupler, drive in a short piece of one-inch pipe. This is the bushing that will center the one-inch dowel in the vertical assembly. One inch is the inner diameter of the pipe.

The bushings must not extend past the center of the couplers, and you may have to grind away the small ridge inside the coupler so the dowel can pass through.

And as it turns out, the ¾-inch PVC tee at the left end of the horizontal arm will fit and rotate nicely inside the one-inch couplers. The screws that fasten the entire assembly to the bulkhead pass through the couplers, the bushings, and the one-inch dowel.

The vertical one-inch dowel must be stationary for the locking and tension control to work. The control device is a piece of ¾-inch dowel that will fit snugly into a ¾-inch threaded cap fitting at one end.

The other end of the ¾-inch horizontal dowel presses against the stationary, one-inch vertical dowel. As you turn the threaded cap, you increase the pressure and tension to keep the swing-out bracket where you want it.

The length of the ¾-inch dowel must be fairly precise. It will depend on the length of the primary arm. If you cut it a bit short, add stainless washers under the cap. Pennies will also work. The T fitting at the base end of the horizontal arm fits into the couplers and rotates in them. Lubricate those rotation points with a little silicone spray.

And leave enough cable free to make the entire swing.

Materials Needed

- Eight-inch piece of one-inch hardwood dowel
- Approx. 12-inch piece of ¾-inch hardwood dowel
- Approx. 12 inches of ¾-inch PVC pipe
- One four-way ¾-inch PVC tee
- Two ¾-inch PVC tees
- One ¾-inch PVC elbow
- One ¾-inch PVC connector, slip to thread
- One threaded ¾-inch PVC cap
- Two one-inch PVC slip pipe connectors
- Approx. four inches, one-inch PVC pipe
- Two #10 and five #8 stainless steel screws
- Four-inch square wooden platform

Installing a Windlass

After a difficult anchor retrieval, the first mate and I decided it was time to add another deck hand for *Prime Time* — an anchor windlass — for our 2002 Catalina 28 Mark II **(below)**.

I chose a Lewmar V700 for its size, good reviews, and price. The local West Marine matched the lowest price I found online ($625).

The installation required some fairly complex carpentry. It can be done with hand power tools, but my table saw, drill press, and router were extremely helpful.

I learned that you can download the entire owner's manual for the Lewmar V700 at:

http://www.lewmar.com/Product-literature.asp.

I did this to get a better idea of what it would take to install it, and to make sure it was right for my boat.

One of the major issues for a vertical-drop windlass is having enough room below decks to store the anchor rode as it comes in. Lewmar says this model needs at least 12 inches below the windlass.

Here's the anchor locker **(above)** with wiring and side supports for the windlass platform in place. But I didn't fasten the side supports to the wall of the locker until after several other steps were completed.

Construction Sequence

I cut the lid of the anchor locker laterally (port to star-board) into three equal 12-inch pieces. The windlass was mounted on the center section.

I hinged the fore and aft sections so they can swing open independently. This gives me access to the locker from either end for installation, maintenance, the wind-lass switch, and any possible rode tangle.

Each of those opening sections should have two hing-es to maintain their alignment. I was able to find exact matches for the original hinges at a local marine surplus store for $4 each

Beware Look-Alike Hinges

Be aware that two hinges, even though they look alike, may not swing the same way.

I ran into a problem with the new aft hinge on the forward section. I discovered there is metal embedded in the fiberglass there to add strength for the bow cleat. I was unable to drill into the metal.

So the forward section has only one functioning hinge. I left the second hinge glued there for the sake of appearance.

I have not yet had to open the forward section to deal with anchor rode problems. If I were starting this project again, I would cut the lid in half, rather than into three pieces.

In the photo at the beginning of this project, notice how I cut out the top of the original chain chute so the new chain would not scrape on it. Because I was concerned about the section maintaining its strength, I screwed a section of half-inch cutting board underneath.

To cut the lid, I made some adapters to hold it straight for my table saw. The lid is convex, which made it difficult to cut a straight line. The cut exposed the wood in the fiberglass sandwich that forms the lid. I weatherproofed that cut with a coat of epoxy.

Starboard for the Windlass Platform

I used 1½-inch thick King Starboard® to build a reinforcing pad under the middle section of the lid where the windlass was mounted. This is critical to insure strength.

There will be major force pulling the windlass toward the bow. Because the locker space is triangular, if you fit the reinforcement pad properly, the pad below the locker lid becomes a wedge in that triangle.

Instead of the mounting screws in the side walls, the triangular locker will take most of the force. I cut my pad 13 inches wide, fore to aft, so it extends a half-inch under both forward and aft sections of the lid when they close.

The pad also serves as a water barrier for the cuts between sections. I chose Starboard for the pad because it's strong, easier to work than wood, and will not rot or warp.

The thickest Starboard I could find was ¾-inch. So I cut two pieces and screwed them together, to make my pad 1½ inches thick.

Another fine point that adds strength – the sides of the anchor locker are tapered. They slant inward at nine degrees off vertical.

If you can cut the pad to fit that side angle (as well as the horizontal triangle) you will achieve maximum strength by giving the pad more surface pushing against the locker walls.

Clamp the lid and the two pieces of starboard together to make sure they fit. In my anchor locker, about one inch of the 1½-inch pad is down in the locker space, lodged against the side walls. Make sure the fore and aft hinged sections will be clear to open and close.

Like all cabinet work, this job requires a lot of trial fitting and slight trimming to make everything fit as tightly as possible. If your pad is not exactly flush with the walls of the locker (as mine was not on one side) use a shim to fill that space.

The bulk of the force on the windlass will be from straight ahead but there will also be some upward force when the windlass is in operation. Be sure to strongly anchor the reinforcing pad to the side walls.

A ledge on each side of angle iron (aluminum or stainless steel) is the obvious way to do this, but it won't fit the tapered walls very well. I have not had good luck changing the bend in 90-degree angled metal.

So I came up with a better way. I used four-inch stainless door hinges. They're very strong and they swing to fit exactly the angle between the horizontal reinforcement pad and the tapered side walls of the locker.

To mark where you'll drill for the mounting screws for the hinges, put the pad in place and then clamp the middle section of the locker lid to it, just as it would be installed.

When you're sure everything is positioned properly, hold the hinges below the pad so they are in place against both the bottom of the pad and sides of the locker.

Then mark the hinge screw holes in the pad where the bolts would go through vertically to fasten the pad to each hinge. Don't mark the holes for the side walls yet.

Remove the pad and drill the vertical screw holes carefully, either with a drill press or portable drill accessory that insures vertically plumb holes.

It is nearly impossible to drill vertically plumb holes freehand, and they *must* be plumb for your windlass and mounting bolts to fit properly.

To bolt the hinges to the pad, I used flat-head ¼-inch bolts two inches long. These were countersunk into the top of the pad. They must be countersunk for the pad to fit tightly under the original lid.

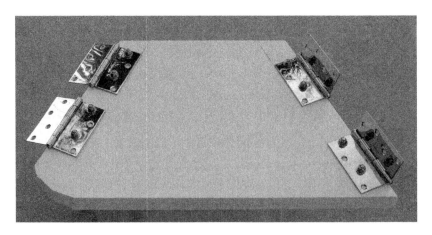

This photo shows the reinforcing pad, upside down, with mounting hardware installed. The center of the lid is convex. More on that in a moment.

With all the hinges bolted securely to the pad, put it in place, once more clamped to the lid as it will be when it's installed. Now carefully mark the holes in the hinges where screws will fasten them to the sides of the locker.

At first, I had planned to fasten the hinges on the sides with quarter-inch bolts. But that would have required cutting a large deck plate into each side so the nut could be held on the backside while the bolt was tightened.

Screwing the Hinges to the Walls

Since there will be little upward force on the assembly and no force to pull the fasteners out of the wall, I mounted the hinges to the walls with #10 stainless screws and a ¾-inch fender washer.

I used hex-head screws. They're much easier to install and remove. Almost all the stress when the anchor is pulling will be toward the bow.

The smaller screws also provide more latitude in having the mounting holes in exactly the right place.

The fender washer under the head of each screw creates more friction against the hinge to improve its holding power. You can see the screw heads and fender washers in the anchor locker photo on the second page of this chapter.

Next, I dealt with the space between the convex fiberglass lid and the flat reinforcement pad.

I placed the lid upside down on a table and used wedges to carefully level it.

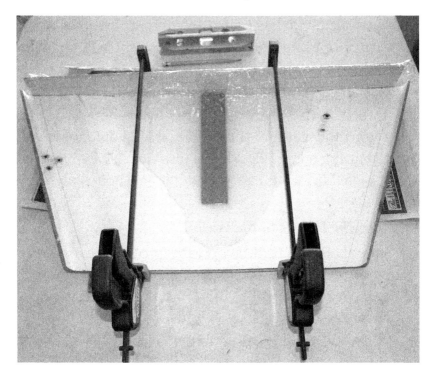

I clamped a thin piece of wood **(above)** against the wider side of the lid, where the concavity was most pronounced. I used very thin wood, thinking that if it got epoxied to the lid, it would be easy to sand it off.

I covered the wood strip in Saran wrap to prevent the epoxy from sticking to it. That worked wonderfully. I marked where the epoxy level should be at the center of the lid.

When I poured the epoxy into the concave lid space, it leveled out to create a flat surface to later bolt against the reinforcement pad. I did this in three pours, embedding a carpenter's shim at the center to help make the thickness more exact.

It's better to add epoxy a little at a time. The more you pour, the more heat will be generated in the curing process.

Don't use newspaper under the lid (as I did) to catch any epoxy drip. The newspaper was epoxied to my anchor lid. It took a lot of patient chipping to remove it later without leaving a scar.

I should have positioned the lid so it hung over the end of the table, with newspaper on the floor to catch drips.

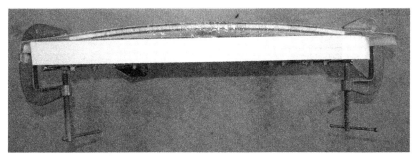

Epoxy Fills Space Between Lid and Platform

Other than that, the epoxy solved my concern that bolting the windlass to the lid might flatten its convexity.

Now bolt the pad and center lid section into place in the anchor locker. I found the easiest sequence was to disconnect the hinges from the pad and mount the hinges to the locker walls first, leaving the screws loose.

Then I put the pad in place, pushing its mounting bolts through the holes in the hinges and putting a lock nut on them underneath. At this point, leave all screws and nuts loosely fastened so you can move the pad slightly to fit everything in place.

Put all three sections of the lid in place to make sure the fore and aft sections will properly swing up with the center lid section permanently bolted in place

You'll now have to decide whether you will cut the circles and bore the mounting holes with the lid center section in place.

I decided I could be more accurate if I removed the center section and used the windlass mounting template to mark the reinforcement pad, because it's flat and the holes can be cut more accurately.

I drilled pilot holes for the windlass mounting bolts and circles in the flat reinforcement pad from the top, using an accessory to make sure the drill was vertically plumb.

This windlass has three mounting bolts and two overlapping circles — one for the motor to be mounted below and another where incoming rope and chain will be dropped into the anchor locker.

With all the pilot holes drilled in the pad from the top, I clamped the lid back in place and, using the pilot holes in the pad as a jig, drilled *from the bottom* and up through the lid.

This way, I could be sure the bolts would be vertical as they passed through both the lid and the pad. It took an extra-long 1/8-inch bit to drill through the pad and the lid section.

I then removed the assembly, unclamped the lid, and cut the two circles in the pad using a 2 1/2-inch hole saw and a circle-cutting adapter for my router.

With the lid detached from the pad and clamped to two sawhorses, I was able to cut those circles the same way. I had expected the convex lid to be more difficult than it was. I then drilled the three windlass mounting bolt holes in both the lid and pad, using the pilot holes made in the step above.

Both the large cutouts could be made with a jig saw but would not be nearly as neat as those cut with a hole saw and router. Because neither is visible once the windlass is installed, my fetish for neat circles may not matter.

Put the lid and pad back in place on the boat and bolt the windlass on, making sure the assembly fits well. The windlass mounting bolts clamp the lid to the reinforcement pad. You will probably need to do some slight work on the mounting bolt holes for the windlass to drop into place.

The windlass comes with a rubber gasket that is designed to eliminate any problem with the convex lid. But if your lid convexity is greater than mine, you may have to shim the windlass and use sealant around the base to make it weatherproof.

Electrical wiring

The installation manual says the power supply for the windlass should come straight from your starter battery, rather than going through your electrical panel. This is because the windlass might draw enough amperage to shut down your entire electrical system.

Connecting to the starter battery is recommended because you will almost always have the engine and alternator running when you operate the windlass.

One of your most challenging tasks will be hiding the wiring as you bring the #8 AWG supply line forward from the battery to a dedicated circuit breaker, and then on to the windlass operating switch. If your windlass is more than 16 feet from the battery, you'll need larger wire to handle the heavy load.

Wire Coming Out of Battery Compartment

Installing a Windlass

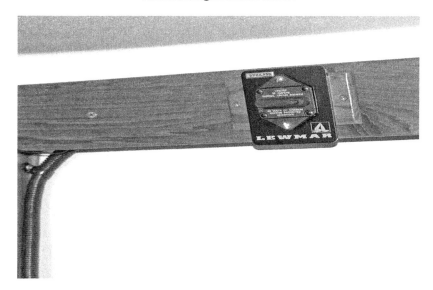

Circuit Breaker in Forward Cabin

Windlass Switch in Anchor Locker

I put the windlass operating switch down inside the anchor locker where it is protected from weather. I also wanted it close by when the windlass is operating so it can be shut down quickly if a problem develops.

You'll need to buy a new chain and anchor rode, unless you can splice your present line to the right-size chain. The windlass requires a G4 or BBB chain and ½-inch line.

Normally, I would have installed a latch on the starboard side of the forward section of the lid to keep it closed. But that's where the hidden steel is embedded in the fiberglass to strengthen the starboard bow cleat.

Because the forward section only has one working hinge, the section is not very strong and can only be used as an inspection port. But how to keep it firmly closed?

I went to a marine store and found a stainless-steel latch that would mount on the sturdy center section. It had a lip that would swing over the forward section and keep it closed. One of these latches was priced at $23.

Toilet Bumpers Make Lid Latches

Instead, I made two latches for a total of $3.40. They're rubber toilet seat bumpers. They work great. Eventually, the sun will destroy them. By then I may come up with another, inexpensive solution.

About the Author

Clarence Jones has always been a writer/mechanic/inventor/tinkerer. He started a school newspaper when he was in the third grade, and built a photographic darkroom in the family bathroom a year later.

He was an accomplished bicycle mechanic in junior high school, then moved up to working on his motor scooter in college. Then his cars.

He built HeathKit® electronics before imported Japanese devices put the build-it-yourself company out of business.

His inventive tinkering skills helped him hide audio recorders, and both still and movie cameras, as investigative reporting tools in both newspapers and TV. Like:

- The 8mm movie camera he smuggled into illegal gambling joints, packaged in a soundproofed lunch box.

- The photo of Florida's Supreme Court Chief Justice throwing dice at a craps table in Las Vegas. All the expenses of the justice's junket were paid by a race track with a pending case before the court.

- The recorded comments of Richard Nixon – about busing students to integrate schools – during a private meeting with Southern delegates at the 1968 Republican Convention.

- Underwater video demonstrating how to escape a car as it sank in a canal.

- The pitches of salesmen pushing worthless high school diplomas on customers who thought they could use them to qualify for a job.
- The theft of a disabled car, left on the shoulder of a road, that was shredded and sold for scrap.

Clarence's graduate degree as a craftsman was earned building a house on the Gulf of Mexico in the Florida Keys. Beginning the job in 1978, he hired two pros and worked with them until the roof was on the house.

Then they left and Clarence spent four years finishing the job, working as a TV reporter in Miami three days a week, as a craftsman/carpenter/electrician/plumber four days a week.

In the Miami and Florida Keys period of his life, he sailed a 25-foot MacGregor. It was followed by a 21-foot MacGregor (chosen because it had been the fastest model in the Miami MacGregor Club races).

When he moved to a landlocked house on Anna Maria Island in 2004, he bought an 18-foot Precision on a trailer. Then a 21-foot Precision.

Weary of rigging the boat, launching it, recovering it, and de-rigging it, he moved to a canal-front house, and abandoned the towing of sailboats.

The first time they sailed the Precision from the dock at the new house – without all that rigging and launching work – his wife's reaction was, "My god, how decadent!"

They now sail an even more decadent, 28-foot Catalina. A magnificent boat for day sailing and weekend cruising. The projects in this book were created over the years for this series of boats.

Some apply only to trailered boats. Most can apply to your boat, no matter its size. Many of the projects and photographs in this book were previously published in sailing magazines.

Clarence's day job now is CEO of Winning News Media, Inc. He and his wife, Ellen Jaffe Jones, work out of a home office. They can jump on their boat and be sailing in Tampa Bay 10 minutes later.

Clarence does on-camera coaching and conducts seminars for government and corporate executives all over America. He published the memoirs of his 30-year reporting career in 2012 — *They're Gonna Murder You — War Stories From My Life At the News Front*.

The title comes from his friends' constant warnings while he was an investigative reporter. His specialties were the Mafia, dirty cops, and crooked politicians.

Before he formed the consulting company and left reporting, Clarence was a newspaper reporter for 16 years (*Florida Times-Union, Jacksonville Journal, Miami Herald*). Between the Jacksonville newspapers and the *Herald*, he was a Nieman Fellow at Harvard University.

He was a television reporter for 14 years (WHAS-TV in Louisville, and WPLG-TV in Miami).

At WPLG, he won four Emmys and became the only reporter for a local TV station to ever win television's equivalent of the Pulitzer Prize three times (duPont-Columbia Awards).

Other Creative Projects

In December, 1968, Clarence was the first reporter in the world to use a computer to crunch data for a series of stories in the *Miami Herald*. The series analyzed 3,400 Criminal Court cases in Miami, from arrest to final disposition. Details about that in his memoirs.

Clarence bought his first desktop computer in 1984. In 2006, he built a computer from scratch for the first time. It was so much easier than he anticipated, he published a how-to book, *Build Your Next PC*.

He also creates and manages websites for his business ventures. Two other e-books he wrote that are currently available ares *Shortcuts for Windows PCs and Webcam Savvy – For the Job or TV News Interview*.

The Best-Seller

His first and best-selling book has been *Winning with the News Media – A Self Defense Manual When You're the Story*. Now in its 8th Edition, it is considered by many to be the "bible" in its field.

He publishes articles frequently on computing, sailing, photography, and home improvement projects. Most are how-to pieces, showing creative, inexpensive ways to do, improve, or make something.

His wife, Ellen, is also a sailor and former TV reporter. She is the author of *Eat Vegan on $4 a Day*, one of the nation's best-selling recipe books for vegetarians.

They have a mixed marriage. Clarence eats meat. Ellen's next book - due for publication in mid-2013 – will be titled *A Divided Kitchen*.

Contact Us

I'd love your feedback. I will make this book a work in progress, adding more projects in future editions. Your ideas and suggestions will be a major factor in that growth and improvement. Here's the contact info:

Clarence Jones

Winning News Media, Inc.

610 Emerald Lane

Holmes Beach, FL 34217-1218

Phone: 941.779.0242

e-mail: cjones@winning-newsmedia.com

Website: www.winning-newsmedia.com

CPSIA information can be obtained
at www.ICGtesting.com
Printed in the USA
LVOW04s0020241115

463845LV00032B/1659/P